HAUNTED
DERBYSHIRE

HAUNTED
DERBYSHIRE

Jill Armitage

The
History
Press

To Anne and David – hope this gives a new dimension to your Derbyshire jaunts.

First published 2009

The History Press
The Mill, Brimscombe Port
Stroud, Gloucestershire, GL5 2QG
www.thehistorypress.co.uk

Reprinted 2016

British Library Cataloguing in Publication Data.
A catalogue record for this book is available from the British Library.

ISBN 978 0 7524 4886 2

Typesetting and origination by The History Press

CONTENTS

INTRODUCTION

G host stories are as old as time, but most people consider them to be just that – stories, works of fiction that are entertaining and a wee bit scary. That's probably not surprising because when these stories get passed on by word of mouth, they lose nothing in the telling. Although it doesn't detract from their appeal, it makes it almost impossible to guarantee their authenticity, but my research has also brought me into contact with countless genuine people who have willingly shared their own amazing, first-hand experiences with me.

I met Val on a computer course and have absolutely no reason to doubt her story. She told me that she is in the habit of taking a glass of water to bed with her and placing it on the bedside table. One night while living in her previous home, she woke and felt for the glass myopically as her sleepy brain tried to work out why it wasn't there. She realised that the bedside table was a different height and on it she discovered that the glass had been replaced by a cup and saucer. Several times after that she would wake to find that the room had slipped back in time. An old wooden cradle would be rocking gently at the foot of her bed which had changed from a modern divan to an iron bed-stead.

Gwen moved into an old cottage in the village where she had lived all her life so she was quite aware that old Joe the previous occupant had died there. This didn't unduly worry her as she had spent her childhood in a haunted house, so she wasn't too concerned to see Joe's shade walking up the stairs one evening.

William is a tough no-nonsense farmer who lives in an old farmhouse which is haunted by a young girl who regularly sits at the end of his bed. Like Val's experience, it is not unusual for him to wake at night to find his room has slipped back to an earlier time.

George had been a complete disbeliever until he had a first-hand experience after which he said, 'He – the ghost – was so real and so close, I could have put my hand in his pocket.'

Many of us experience doors that open by themselves, objects that move, and sounds that can't be identified. We feel draughts, known as psychic breezes. We sense a presence or a strange atmosphere, but because most of us are disbelievers until convinced otherwise, we always look for logical explanations. We explore all avenues to get to the bottom of the mystery, convincing ourselves that there has to be some rational explanation however implausible.

The experiences of Val, Gwen, William and George, like a lot of the other stories in *Haunted Derbyshire* were told to me by privileged people who have been given a glimpse into another dimension. How that happens is a mystery. Despite many tries, no one has been able to explain it satisfactorily. It breaks all the rules of time and space as we know them, and if we look for a rational explanation we won't find it. Something caused these scenarios to become imprinted on time itself, locked into the place where they happened. That is why just occasionally, if the time is right and you let yourself listen, you may hear the echoes, feel the ripples and see the visions as they reach out over the years, but in the meantime, sit back and enjoy *Haunted Derbyshire*, but don't be surprised if you are not alone.

One

HAUNTED HOMES, HALLS & HOSPITALS

The chaperone ghost at Scathin

In the nineteenth century, it was rather unusual for a single woman to buy her own home, yet, according to the deeds of a property near the post office at Scathin, the first person to own that property was a single lady called Emma. Since then, various families have lived there without experiencing anything unusual, but when a single lady called Carol moved in, strange things began to happen.

Carol regularly had female friends staying and all was well, but when male friends stayed, they found great difficulty sleeping and even had their bed-clothes torn off by an unseen presence. Was it Emma who was keeping a motherly eye on Carol and acting as an unseen chaperone? Apparently her predecessor never experienced this, and since Carol has moved out, the invisible chaperone has not struck again.

The tranquil setting of Scathin.

The ghost who vowed to take care of Joan

The first few months of married life for Ron and Joan Webster were spent living with her parents at an old building on Beetwell Street, Chesterfield. What Ron didn't realise until later, was that he was also living with a phantom member of the family too.

One night while in bed, Ron woke to see a figure beginning to materialise at the side of the bed. It was a young man in a black uniform. It was so clear, he could see the riding breeches, the jacket with rows of silver buttons on his chest, wide-cuffed gloves, and a strange black skull-cap with goggles pulled back over it. He beckoned menacingly to Ron before disappearing.

Unsure whether it had been a dream, Ron said nothing about this, but the following night he woke to feel a pair of hands gripping his legs. It felt as though he was being dragged out of bed and there at the bottom of the bed he saw the same apparition. He had the distinct impression that the spectre was trying to scare him away. On the third night, the spectre almost succeeded as it stood there glowering at him. It was then that Ron decided enough was enough and told the family.

Joan admitted that she too had seen the apparition, wearing identical uniform to that described by her husband, and produced photographs of her cousin Jack, who had been killed in the war. His uniform was just as Ron had described; standard wartime issue for dispatch riders. Jack had always said that he would look after Joan and she believed he was doing just that.

The ghost of Church Lady House

When Labour MP Roy Hattersley bought a period property in Great Longstone he was not only buying a little bit of Derbyshire history, he was also acquiring a ghost. Sheffield-born Mr Hattersley has adopted Derbyshire as his home county after falling for the charms of Church Lady House, and wasn't unduly perturbed when told that the property is reputed to be haunted by a ghoulish woman dressed in black. 'If a ghost is the only problem we have, I'll be happy,' he said.

Smokey ghosts

Gordon and Hannah Robinson are non-smokers and when friends and neighbours visit they respect their wishes not to smoke in their home at New Road, Eyam, but how can you stop a ghost from leaving the smell of tobacco all around the house?

'We never actually see the smoke or the ghost,' said Gordon, 'but the smell is unmistakable. We don't mind having a ghost. We first noticed him several years ago when objects started to move mysteriously and a glass chandelier hanging in the living room was several times found lying on the floor totally undamaged. He isn't any trouble and we would hardly notice him if it wasn't for the pipe smoking.'

The antique shop ghost

Geoff Clifton told me a story about a friend of his named Ken who ran an antique shop in a village on the Derbyshire/Leicestershire border. Ken lived behind the shop in this period building which stood in the Market Place.

One evening Geoff was visiting Ken. After spending some time chatting in the dining room, Geoff got up to leave. He walked out of the dining room and down a 25ft passage which led to the front door. He was almost there when he felt a hand on his shoulder and turned, expecting it to be Ken.

To his surprise, there was no one behind him and Ken was just leaving the dining room 20ft away. As Ken passed a dower chest which stood in the passage, he appeared to stumble and fall. He swore under his breath. 'That bloody woman pushed me again.'

Geoff was more intrigued than alarmed as he had previously owned an antique shop at the eighteenth-century canal port of Shardlow. In one of the basement rooms there was a specific cold spot which was definitely not caused by a draught or any rational explanation. The draught theory was tested when Geoff's son stood in the spot with a cigarette lighter and watched the flame burn steadily with no trace of a sideways movement. A look at the building's past revealed nothing; it had been a salt warehouse, a cycle shop, a butcher's and a saddler's. It is now a private house.

From then on, the two men shared their experiences. Both had come to accept the fact that their buildings were haunted. Ken's ghost was decidedly female because he had heard the rustle of skirts. She also made her presence known by making noises like the pages of a book being turned. What both ghostly visitors seemed to have in common was their ability to lift door latches and open doors when there was no one near and no wind or draught to blow them open. Ken told how he would shut his bedroom door, stand back and count to three. The latch would then lift and the door open; it became a source of considerable bemusement, yet there was no logical explanation unless you accept the fact that this ghost just didn't like being shut out of the bedroom.

Please don't close the door

Ghosts that don't like being restricted or banned from any particular place are certainly not rare. Sophia had a flat in a purpose-built block, and a ghost with a similar obsession to Ken's. If she closed the bathroom door before going to bed, she was sure to be troubled in the night, yet if it was left open, nothing happened. This theory was tested out on numerous occasions, both intentionally and accidentally, and the result was always the same. A month after moving out, Sophia had to go back to the flat to collect some things. She knocked and the door was opened by the new occupant, who said, 'Oh, I thought you were the joiner. I need someone to sort out the bathroom door – it just won't stay closed.' It would appear that the ghost had actually found that 'he' could open the door himself. Sophia didn't think she should inform the new resident they had a ghost that liked the bathroom door left open.

The haunted house at Upper Mayfield

Before buying a house, it might be advantageous to ask if it is haunted! In 1994, Andrew and Josie Smith didn't, and four years later made legal history by suing the people who sold them Lowe Cottage because they were not told about the cottage's paranormal past. A civil court in Derby was asked to sit in judgement and if the action against the vendors had been successful, which it wasn't, this would have represented the first time since the Middle Ages that a British court had recognised the existence of ghosts.

Lowes Cottage is a detached, stone-built, three-storey property standing on a hill in Upper Mayfield, a tiny village on the border between Derbyshire and Staffordshire. It was once the servant's quarters to nearby Lowes Farm and has retained some of the original features – cooking range, oak beams and vaulted ceiling, sandstone frame-work and latticed windows.

In May 1994, Andrew who is a joiner and his wife Josie a nurse, agreed to pay £44,000 for the property but could only raise a £41,000 mortgage. They agreed to pay the difference by instalments over the next three years to the owners, two sisters Susan Melbourne and Sandra Podmore. Lowes Cottage had been their family home. They had lived there from being small children and they had inherited it from their father. They maintained throughout that they had never experienced anything strange there.

What should have been a straightforward sale of property was soon to turn into a benchmark legal case acted out in the full glare of the national media spotlight. According to the newspapers, the Smiths had refused to pay a final instalment to the vendors because of the problems they claimed to have endured. As a result, the two sisters launched a county court action to recover the money due. In response the Smiths filed their own counterclaim in the civil courts for the return of £41,000 purchase price for not being told of the cottage's reputation for paranormal activity.

Andrew and Josie Smith were most concerned about the effect on their three children: Lindsey, then aged twelve, Stephen who was five, and one-year-old Daniel. The Smiths claimed their ordeal began shortly after they moved into the cottage in 1994. They started to notice a horrible stench which seemed to move from room to room. The smell filled the house several nights every week but checks on the plumbing drew a blank.

On two occasions Josie woke in the night to find herself unable to move, her body pinned to the bed by some invisible force. She described her experience to a *Daily Mail* reporter:

> I was completely paralysed and it felt as though there was this enormous weight pressing down on me. It was so powerful I had to use all my strength and power to shift it… because it engulfed my whole body, and after a few minutes it left.

The eldest daughter Lindsey experienced strange dreams and the apparition of a young girl in the cottage. During this early period the family found the rooms filling with a thick, heavy fog which was accompanied by an evil presence and dramatic sudden drops in temperature. On one occasion, Andrew ventured upstairs to confront the presence in a bedroom and was overpowered by a nauseating smell. He said 'The fog was so heavy I had a job moving my arms around and it was so thick you could lean on it. I could feel the atmosphere building up by the second and the room felt as if it was about to explode.'

After a year of living in the cottage, the couple approached a spiritualist church for help and brought in the Revd Peter Mockford to bless the house. Temporarily this seemed to lift the oppressive atmosphere, then he placed his hands on the wall in the couple's bedroom and suddenly the walls started running with water. There were no pipes in that wall, it was a hot day, there was no puddle at the bottom and when the water stopped, the walls were dry in ten minutes.

Revd Mockford suggested that the family played religious hymns to exorcise the spirits, but the evil presence failed to respond to this idea. That night the couple were woken by a supernatural cacophony. This included the sound of the hi-fi system playing at full blast while the immersion heater overheated and the cottage filled with a dreadful odour. The hi-fi could only be silenced when the plug was pulled and the next day it was found the fuses on the water heater had blown.

The following night, Andrew claimed he woke with a jolt to find Josie lying on her back with her mouth wide open, kicking her legs violently in the air as if something was throttling the life out of her. She struggled for ages until the spirit left her, then Andrew heard something going up the stairs and it gave a terrible groan that made his hair stand on end. On one occasion, a neighbour claimed a disembodied spirit passed through his body during a visit to the house.

During their four years at the cottage, they had endured poltergeist manifestations of objects flying through the air; heard deep groans, creaking floor-boards and footsteps; failing electrical equipment; acrid smells and sudden, inexplicable drops in temperature. Josie claimed she had seen apparitions of a bound, naked woman, a little boy with piggy eyes and a woman in nineteenth-century costume. The family periodically left the house to escape the hauntings, sleeping on the floor of Andrew's mother's two-bedroom flat. On one of these occasions, the family returned to find their two pet budgies dead 'their faces pressed against the cage in identical positions.'

The priest suggested that in order to put the spirits to rest, they should be identified. This led to a search through records and an appeal to folk memory. They heard that a young milkmaid called Elaine had been imprisoned, abused and murdered in the cellar of Lowes Cottage in the nineteenth century. Searches in the local record office established that a fifteen-year-old girl called Elaine Harring had indeed lived in the servant quarters which became Lowes Cottage in 1861.

Also there was a vague story about a young boy who was reputed to have hanged himself from the rafters. Could this be Joseph Phillips, identified as a cow-lad at the farm? There was no record to suggest a murder or a suicide had befallen either Elaine Harring or Joseph Phillips, but unconvinced, Andrew began to dig up parts of the garden believing they could have been buried there. He found nothing.

In May 1998, two ghostbusters from Ashbourne visited the house in an attempt to find evidence to back up the couple's claims. Their recording equipment picked up an odd male voice and their infra-red camera picked up a strange white mist that engulfed one of the bedrooms. By 1998 when the family moved out, the cottage had been exorcised five times by a Church of England priest who has described it as 'a demonic house – the most severe case he had ever been asked to deal with'.

But the evidence was considered insufficient at the January 1999 court hearing. Judge Peter Stretton in his scathing ten-minute summary of the case said 'this house is not haunted and never has been haunted. The noises, damp and smell were more likely to be created by man than by ghosts.'

The Lowes Cottage case was in fact the latest in a series of courtroom findings which have highlighted the reluctance of the judiciary to rule upon the existence or otherwise of the supernatural. In 1989, a council-house tenant in Nottinghamshire sought a judicial review to the local authority's decision not to re-house his family who claimed their house was infested by a poltergeist. In New York however, the existence of ghosts has been legally established as a result of a court ruling. In 1991, the State Appellate Court set a legal precedent that vendors must inform potential buyers if a house is haunted or face having to return the deposit.

The Smiths subsequently put the cottage back on the market at £50,000 with no reference to any hauntings in the estate agent's literature, and in April 1999 it was bought by London businessman Tim Clinton who is also a member of the Churches Fellowship for Physical and Spiritual Studies who paid £56,000. Mr Clinton has promised a fresh start for any troubled spirits that might be hanging around.

Lowes Cottage, described by a Church of England priest as a 'demonic house'.

The bells of Rosehill

This haunting dates from 1830, but came to light when an article appeared in the *Nottingham and Derby Notes and Queries* in 1897 after a lady discovered the story in an old book belonging to her family. The information had been passed on by her great uncle Mr James Ashwell and concerned the time when he resided at Rosehill, Chesterfield. He had lived there for only a few months when the bells in the house, intended to be used to summon servants, began to ring for no apparent reason.

Mr Ashwell initially blamed the servants, but they were later absolved from blame after being deliberately locked in the library prior to and while the bells rang. In fact, rather understandably, servants frequently left in alarm. Unable to remedy the situation, new bells were installed, but they too continued the mysterious ringing. Changing the position of the bells made no difference. In whatever order they were placed, they always rang in their self-appointed order.

Even when the wires were severed the ringing continued. Electrical and wind experiments were tried in order to explain the behaviour of the bells but without success. All the bells were hung well out of human reach and despite thorough investigation there was no evidence of tampering. The phantom campanology continued for eighteen months and was never solved.

This kind of haunting has all the markings of poltergeist activity – channels of unseen energy that are able to move small objects, create sounds and smells. Some poltergeist outbursts act almost like psychic temper tantrums. A teenage child or a person in an odd state of mind (depression, emotional outbursts and fits of temper) within a location that has a powerful energy field is usually found to be at the root of the problem, and as the state of mind changes, the problem usually ceases.

Although this magnificent house was pulled down in the 1930s its name still lives on in the area which is now the site of the Chesterfield Town Hall. What caused the bells to ring is still a mystery but if the staff at the town hall hear bells ringing and it's not the telephone, beware!

Ogston Hall ghost

Ogston is now best known for its 210-acre reservoir that nestles in the Amber valley, yet the area was first mentioned in the Domesday Book when it was held by the Deincourt family. In the fourteenth century it passed to the Revell family and remained with them until 1727 when the last male heir died. Through marriage it passed to the Turbutt family whose continuous occupation lasted 246 years. It is still a private estate owned by the Wakefield family.

The family seat is Ogston Hall which stands on a prominence of high ground to the south of the reservoir. It has been built in four distinct stages and displays four very different styles of architecture, the oldest section being the west wing dating back to medieval times. It is this wing that is said to be haunted by one of the last Revells – Leonard.

In the 1880s, the west wing was used as sleeping quarters for the female servants and around 1881 two maids were woken in the middle of the night by the sound of someone dragging a heavy object across the floor. Thinking it was an intruder, they alerted the male servants who slept across the courtyard.

A search was made in the house but no one was discovered. The shouts of the hysterical females to the men servants could have disturbed the intruder yet this was discounted, despite the fact that the doors between the west wing and the rest of the house, which were always meticulously locked by W.G. Turbutt at night, were found unlocked. Everyone was questioned, yet no member of the household had touched them.

Many years later, Don Lees the Ogston estate gamekeeper stayed at the Hall while the family were away, and he not only heard the ghost, he also saw it. The story that circulated was that this

Rosehill, prior to demolition in the 1930s.

Rosehill, now the site of the town hall.

Ogston Hall – the haunt of Leonard Revell.

unaccountable disturbance was the ghost of Leonard Revell, who had been hanged in 1723 for the murder of his servant in the west wing of Ogston Hall. Is the ghostly sound the re-enactment of this foul deed as Leonard Revell drags the corpse of his servant across the floor?

Tissington Hall

The charming estate village of Tissington has grown harmoniously around its village green, and unlike many villages the focal point of the settlement is not the church which stands on the high ground overlooking the houses, but the long, low Hall set in the centre of the village. Its stately grandeur is emphasised by its fine iron gates wrought by the Derby smith, Robert Bakewell.

Tissington is mentioned as Tizinctun in the Domesday Book in the possession of Henry de Ferrers. Nicholas FitzHerbert, a younger son of the Derbyshire FitzHerbert family, acquired Tissington in the 1460s by marriage and the family has lived there ever since. The present Hall was built by Francis FitzHerbert around 1609 with later additions and major changes in 1900.

Tissington Hall's tormented souls date back to a time way before a building was there. A Viking craftsman has been sensed in the residual energy. It is very possible that back in the Dark Ages, petty criminals were held in the individual cells in the cellar, as scratching sounds have been heard there and a man in black has been seen. Doors in the cellar are known to close of their own accord.

The handsome dining room was previously a kitchen and is haunted by the spirits of a man and woman – possibly man and daughter or husband and wife – who date from the Civil War period. There is a lot of laughter but the gentleman is very authoritative. According to mediums, his name is William FitzHerbert and he feels he should be there. During the Civil War the FitzHerberts supported the Royalist cause and the family were lucky to escape the destruction of their home by the Parliamentarian troops under Cromwell.

But possibly the most poignant spirit is believed to be that of Wilhelmina who died here in a fire in 1862. She accidentally set fire to the bedclothes, her nightgown went up in flames and

Tissington Hall hosts a number of tormented souls.

she ran around, demented with pain. Eventually her sister dowsed the flames and put out the fire, but Wilhelmina was dreadfully burnt. The fire happened on 20 August but she lingered on in excruciating pain until 15 September. Her anger is so strong she now haunts the building. Most activity is in bedroom four but her footsteps have been heard in the upstairs corridor where raps, taps, sighs and humming noises plus the occasional wail have also been heard.

When engineers were called in recently to do a survey, they filmed video footage and on the section of film taken in what has become known as the haunted bedroom, the image of a full length portrait was seen falling to the floor. There was no such painting in the room at the time.

Dr Stokes' house

New Square has perhaps changed less than most areas of Chesterfield over the years. On its northern side is a building previously known as Soresby Hall and later the Manor House. It was once occupied by a Ladies Seminary run by Miss Topey, and during the early years of the nineteenth century it was the home of Dr Stokes, described as a 'worthy and eminent botanist'.

It was during this time that his wife saw a small child in the corridor and thinking it was some infant that had wandered in off the street, she reached out to take the tiny hand and was horrified when her hand went straight through the ethereal body.

Another occupant heard the sound of clanking chains walk across the hall and into the dining room. Thinking to imprison the fettered phantom in there, she quickly locked the door, but this proved to be no deterrent; the apparition clanked noisily out again. Another lady was reading the Bible when she was suddenly confronted by an apparition. She promptly threw her Bible at it and the apparition faded away.

More recently the building has become the banking premises of the National Provincial Bank and since the 1970s the Yorkshire Bank, but the paranormal activity has not ceased. Most of the activity seems to be centralised around the manager's office which was undoubtedly the previous

Left: *Dr Stokes' house in New Square in the nineteenth century.*

Below: *Dr Stokes' house in New Square is now the Yorkshire Bank.*

dining room on the right of the front door. Computer terminals in there malfunction and one member of the banking staff told me that whenever she went into that room, the pictures were always hanging on a slant despite the number of times she straightened them. Was this a playful ghost? The building was completely refurbished and reopened on 17 May 1999 and the room previously used by the manager was allocated to be used to house the mechanics of the mini-bank, but did this stop the activity?

Not according to a lady who services the mini-bank. She has experienced some very bizarre incidents when filling it up. Other members of staff and customers have seen the queue dividers in the main banking hall move despite no one being near, so next time you're in the queue don't be surprised if you're nudged by an impatient ghost.

The Cottage Hospital in Lea, where Florence had her first experience of tending the sick, is now the Jug and Glass Inn.

Florence Nightingale of Lea

Lea's most famous resident is undoubtedly Florence Nightingale, the 'Lady with the Lamp', who brought nursing out of the Dark Ages and made it a serious and respected profession.

On their marriage, her wealthy parents Fanny and William Nightingale moved into Lea Hall, the previous home of Peter Nightingale, William's grandfather, but soon they were off on the Grand Tour. During the next two years they produced two daughters, Parthenope (born in Naples) and Florence born on 12 May 1820 and also named after the place of her birth. Returning to Lea Hall, Fanny decided this was too old, too small and too cold, so Lea Hurst was built.

Florence's father William Nightingale was born William Shore, but changed his name to inherit the fortune of his uncle Peter Nightingale who owned land, property and mineral rights in the area. Peter also built a house and an adjoining row of cottages at Lea for use as a hospital for his workers. This is now the Jug and Glass Inn and is probably where Florence's interest in nursing began. Florence felt that her own affluence was wrong when there was so much poverty and suffering around and she started helping the local villagers where there was evidence of malnutrition, disease, poverty and poor sanitation.

Lea Hurst remained in the Nightingale family until Louis Nightingale died in 1940. In 1951, it was presented to the Royal Surgical Aid Society and it became a home for the elderly. Residents and staff here have reported seeing Florence's ghost wandering along a top corridor and down the stairs. Is she responsible for the sighs, the creaking floor-boards, the strange antiseptic smells and the sudden, inexplicable drops in temperature felt at the Jug and Glass? It is very likely because many people believe that the caring spirit of Florence Nightingale still wanders round her familiar haunts in Lea.

The ghostly castle

Riber Castle is now a brooding ruin that dominates the Matlock skyline from its 853ft-high perch. It was built to a design by John Smedley, a local hosiery manufacturer who became so involved in the hydropathic and medicinal qualities of Matlock's water, that he started the Matlock Hydros.

Riber Castle, the haunt of a lady in blue.

It was John Smedley who was responsible for turning Matlock into a prosperous spa town.

Riber Castle was built as his family home, between 1862-8 at a cost of £60,000 and because of its remote and inaccessible position, the castle had its own well and gas-producing plant for lighting the lavish interior. When John Smedley died in 1874, his widow Caroline continued to live there. In 1888 the building was sold and became a boy's school until 1929. It was never to be lived in again and fell into gradual decline. The Matlock Urban Council purchased it for £1,150 and for a time it was used as a store for the War Office, but it was later left to become a ruined shell.

In 1962, it was purchased by a group of zoologists for £540 and until the end of the twentieth century the buildings and surrounding area were used as a zoo. In recent years a move has been made to revamp the site and build new housing on what has become known as Smedley's Folly, but will the spectres that haunt the site approve?

The most prolific ghost is said to be a lady in blue who patrols the grounds and wanders through the empty corridors and rooms. One woman who saw her while walking her dogs described her as having untidy hair, a gentle expression and sad, shadowed eyes. Could this be Caroline Smedley who, although given little recognition, took an active part in the hydropathic establishment alongside her husband.

At times people have also seen a figure in military uniform who not only marches round the walls, but through them too. He was witnessed by Mr and Mrs Linnett in 1973.

A ghostly hand at Taddington Hall

Taddington Hall is one of those large village houses which was probably the home of some prosperous yeoman in centuries gone by. It is a handsome stone-built house facing squarely down towards the main street of Taddington. There are two ghosts that frequent the building; one is a tipsy farmer who once owned Taddington Hall.

It was his regular practice to ride into Bakewell every Monday to attend the market. He usually returned home at dusk very much the worse for drink. One Monday evening, the farmer's wife heard the horse enter the yard as usual and waited for her husband to stagger in. He did, but to her horror, he walked through the door without opening it, leaving the undamaged door intact. Shortly afterwards, some men arrived to say that her husband's dead body had been found at the bottom of Bakewell Hill. Ever since, his ghost has reputedly re-enacted that last homecoming, every Monday evening at dusk.

It would seem that this ghost has company. In the early hours of a snowy, winter morning in 1947, Bill Furness, a local farmer got up to check on a sick mare housed in a field opposite Taddington Hall. He had previously made arrangements with Lt-Col. Edgar Smalley that if the mare was no better, he could use the Hall's stables to give the mare warmth and shelter. He made the decision to do just that, but the mare was reluctant to enter her new quarters and made every effort to bolt out of the stable yard and back to her field. Struggling to calm her, the farmer heard a quiet, composed voice from the gateway saying 'Whoa! Whoa there!'

This decidedly helped to calm the mare and the farmer was able to get her into the stable before he went to thank his unknown helper. But where had he gone? Not only was there no sign of the man, the only prints in the snow were his and his horse's. It is thought that the unseen helper was a man called Isaac, one of two brothers who had run a small hessian factory in what is now the Hall's saddle room and in the arched cellar below. The brother's quarrelled and Isaac was found in the cellar with his throat cut, a victim of fratricide.

Platchetts House

Harold and Norah Kirby lived at Platchetts House, Breedon Hill from 1952 until it was demolished in 1966. One evening Harold and Norah Kirby and their other children had gone to bed leaving their nineteen-year-old daughter Pat studying downstairs. As usual they had left the landing light on, with instructions to Pat to turn it off when she went to bed. Some time later, they heard footsteps come up the stairs and they waited for the landing light to be switched off but after waiting quite a time, thinking Pat had forgotten, Norah got up to do so. She peeped into Pat's room but found it empty. Rather surprised, she went downstairs and found Pat had fallen asleep in a chair.

Norah's mother was told of the incident and she admitted that on a number of occasions while staying at Platchetts House, she too had heard the footsteps, although instead of walking up the stairs they were always going down. They would then walk along the stone path under the window. She had heard them so many times, she had fallen into the habit of counting them and always there were eleven steps down the stairs, then thirteen steps outside. Norah's aunt had also experienced this while staying at Platchett's House and she too confirmed that she had heard the same number – eleven down the stairs and thirteen outside.

The family could find no explanation for this, but the mystery deepened when the house was demolished by the quarry company, and human bones were found buried in the garden.

Jacobean House

As its name would imply, this magnificent building was constructed in Derby around 1676 when the Jacobites were on the throne of England. Part of the building, which originally had five gables, was demolished in the Victorian era to make an exit through to Becket Street. Apart from that, the existing building would be recognisable to the Victorians, particularly as a phantom horse and carriage is regularly seen waiting in the Wardwick outside the house.

Mrs Hall, who formerly worked at the house, told how she was in the upstairs rooms when she felt someone brush past. She turned immediately to see a lady in a blue dress walking out of the door and down the stairs. Mrs Hall followed but the lady had disappeared. She asked colleagues if they had seen anyone but no one had. Several days later, she saw her again walking up the stairs, but this time over her blue dress she wore a white shawl. Again the lady vanished, but on this occasion others had also seen her. Once word of this got out, other people working in the house admitted to

Jacobean House, Derby.

seeing her too, always in the area of the stairs. They all agreed she looked so gentle and kind, and was not threatening in any way, in fact she became so much a part of the house that when things went missing, as they often did, the 'blue lady' usually took the blame.

The helper at The Grange

The Grange on Southgate, Eckington is now a residential home for the elderly and although meals are taken at the normal times, in the middle of the night it is not unusual to smell bacon frying. The appetising smell appears in various rooms and corridors, but it's not some form of midnight snack, because no one can trace its source.

In the late 1980s Susan Herbert was a regular volunteer at The Grange, and along with a team of other volunteers, often supervised jumble sales and other charity events to raise funds. On one occasion, with the help of a colleague, Susan was carrying boxes of jumble up a flight of stairs into storage. The two women chatted as they moved the boxes and after several trips, Susan realised that her companion who was following her up the stairs was strangely quiet. She could still hear her breathing heavily from the exertion, and felt her close behind her, but when she reached the top of the stairs and turned round, Susan was alone. Her colleague was still downstairs, so who had followed her?

The ghosts of Renishaw Hall

Renishaw Hall on the south-eastern outskirts of Eckington has been the Derbyshire seat of the Sitwell family for over 350 years and is now the home of Sir Reresby Sitwell, 7th Baronet of

Renishaw Hall.

Renishaw and Lady Sitwell. But this sixty-five-room stately home can also claim its fair share of paranormal residents causing the 'Duke's Landing' on the first floor to be dubbed by the family 'Ghost Passage'.

'I've never seen them, but they can worry the guests,' says Sir Reresby. 'We've had the place exorcised several times. The first was done by a Catholic Monsignor Alfred Gilbey, and the next by a spiritual friend of mine, but I don't think it did any good. David the resident butler thinks he heard something odd a few weeks ago in the Ghost Passage'.

One of the busiest of the Renishaw ghosts is believed to be Henry Sacheverell, a sickly child who drowned aged thirteen in 1726. The last of the Sacheverells, his portrait entitled The Boy in Pink, hangs in the magnificent dining room of Renishaw Hall. He has also become known as the kissing ghost because he has a rather surprising penchant for nestling up to lady guests and waking them with kisses from beyond the grave.

In 1885, when Sir George Sitwell, Sir Reresby's grandfather celebrated his twenty-fifth birthday, a large party was held at Renishaw Hall. Amongst the guests were Dr Tait, the Archbishop of Canterbury and his daughter. That night Miss Tait retired to the room which she had been given at the top of the staircase, but woke several hours later trembling with fright. She was alone in the room yet someone had given her three cold kisses.

Miss Tait ran through to the bedroom of Sir George's sister Florence and managed to blurt out the story. Twenty-seven-year-old Florence Sitwell was very sympathetic and understanding, because the very same thing had happened to her when she slept there. Miss Tait was too distressed to return to the room and spent the rest of the night on a temporary bed made on the couch in Florence's room.

The following day, Mr Turnbull the estate agent went to the house, and in a light hearted manner, Sir George told him about the ghostly occurrences of the previous night. Mr Turnbull turned pale. 'You may joke about it Sir George,' he said, 'but when you lent us Renishaw Hall for our honeymoon,

Did Lady Baden-Powell experience the Renishaw Ghost?

Miss Crane, the sister of Walter Crane the artist, a long-time friend who had been at school with my wife, came to stay with us. She had the same room and exactly the same experience.'

Some time after this, Sir George decided to rebuild the staircase. His cousin Mr F.I. Thomas had suggested that if one wall of the room at the top of the stairs was knocked down, the staircase could be enlarged. Work commenced, but very soon a rather macabre discovery was made. Under the floorboards of the room where Miss Tait and the other ladies had experienced the ghostly kisses, they found a coffin. It was of early eighteenth century design and workmanship, fastened to the joists under the floor boards by iron cramps. It had no lid; the floor boards had acted as a lid. There were no bones in the coffin, but it had certain definite marks which suggested that it had once contained a body.

Twenty years later, in September 1909, Lady Ida Sitwell, Sir George's wife was lying on a sofa in the upstairs drawing room, talking to friends after dinner. Facing the open door, she saw a grey-haired woman, wearing a white cap, and something like a two tone blue crinoline, walk along the passage with a very slow, curious gliding motion as if wishing to escape notice. Lady Sitwell thought it was the housekeeper and called out to her by name. There was no reply as the figure headed straight towards the head of the old staircase which had been removed twenty years previously. One lady guest described how it had glided into the darkness and melted away at the point where the doorway had previously led from the staircase to the haunted room. A full-scale search revealed nothing.

These incidents at Renishaw Hall came to my attention when I was writing *The Derbyshire Childhood of Olave, Lady Baden-Powell GBE*. This is a name that will be familiar to Scouts and Guides worldwide yet few know that Olave St Clair Soames was born at Stubbing Court, Wingerworth on 22 February 1889. The Soames family moved to West House, Chesterfield then in 1895, to Renishaw Hall for two years while the Sitwells were in residence at Scarborough. Sir George contested seven elections as conservative candidate for Scarborough and was twice returned as MP.

It was during this time while the Soames family were in residence that a further incident occurred on that same staircase. The result might have been tragic as Olave fell over the banister of the stairs onto a sky light and only narrowly avoided plummeting to almost certain death. Mrs Katharine Soames, Olave's mother kept a dairy and here is a short extract pertaining to the incident.

How the child fell over, how she could have jumped high enough to overbalance herself is a mystery. We can only gather that the others heard a crash and rushing back, Auriol clung to Olave's legs through the rail – and saved her from a hideous fall of 30ft to a stone floor below.

Could this incident also have been connected with the Renishaw Hall ghost or was it just a coincidence?

The ghost of George Stephenson at Tapton House

Tapton House was the much loved home of George Stephenson, the 'Railway King', who leased it in 1838 until his death on 12 August 1848. Such was the respect in which he was held, both nationally and locally, that on the day of his funeral, all the shops of Chesterfield were closed. He was laid to rest beneath the altar in Holy Trinity church, Newbold Road, but 'laid to rest' are inappropriate words considering the number of times he has been seen since, and the most sightings have been at Tapton House.

In the 1920s two young girls were playing in the grounds of the empty mansion. To their delight they found an old coach in the otherwise empty coach house and climbed inside to play. After a while they became aware of an old gentleman standing in a corner against the wall watching them. He was of medium height but appeared taller because of the tall, stove pipe hat he was wearing.

Fearing a reprimand, they left in a hurry and ran home. They hesitantly told of their experience and much to their surprise, the father of one of the girls was most interested. He had been a footman to Sir Charles Markham, a previous owner of the house and he too had seen the ghost on several occasions. It was believed to be the great man himself, George Stephenson.

From 1931-1993 Tapton House was a school, and apparently there were many sightings during this time. On one occasion, a caretaker was sweeping a corridor on the first floor when she was disturbed by a male voice reproaching her with the words 'You didn't bring my water up today.' She found herself facing a stranger dressed in an outdated style, although everything else about him was perfectly normal.

He repeated the complaint and the lady expressed a rather bewildered apology as she turned to go back down the corridor. Meeting her husband, she told him of the strange encounter and they both returned to the spot, but it was now deserted. As the stranger hadn't passed them, the only means of leaving the corridor was through a door which the caretaker confirmed was still locked.

Left: Bronze statue of George Stephenson, the Railway King, outside Chesterfield railway station.

Below: Plaque at Tapton House.

Later, the head teacher produced an album of old photographs and pictures. The lady was asked to look at the portraits and see if any were familiar. Without hesitation, she singled out a portrait of George Stephenson.

After a considerable revamp, in 1994 Tapton House was taken over by the Chesterfield College of Further and Higher Education who are still there today, but the sightings did not stop. Over the last few years there have been reports of doors mysteriously opening and closing, and masculine footsteps on the corridor. On one occasion, the footsteps were accompanied by the sound of a child skipping alongside. A former cleaner felt his presence so strongly she always said 'Good morning George' every time she walked into the room where he died, and a former student told me that while it was a school there was a portrait of George Stephenson that hung in the hall, and the eyes followed you around. This may have been childish imagination and the portrait is no longer there to check it out, but there is a strong feeling that George Stephenson still keeps an eye on his old home.

Left: *The sumptuous interior of the library as George Stephenson would have known it.*

Below: *Tapton House, where the presence of George Stephenson is still felt.*

Sensitive Children

Children and animals are said to be particularly sensitive to paranormal activity. Former occupants of Haywood Farm, Grindleford often found their son chuckling at the antics of a little man in his bedroom. As only he could see the little man they put it down to his active imagination until one evening they saw the electric light swinging and the boy said that the little man had just hit it with his stick. On another occasion, although there was no breeze, the curtain kept billowing out. According to their son, the little man was pulling them about.

The residents of a cottage in north-west Derbyshire said how his daughter saw a little girl with golden ringlets playing with Christmas decorations in her room.

After the death of a Tideswell man his favourite chair was placed in the bedroom of the man's small grandchild, but after a time, the child started getting very upset saying he didn't like the old man sitting watching him. His parents then realised that their son was in the presence of the grandfather he was too young to remember, they felt that the best course of action was to burn the chair and cut the link between the living and dead.

Wingerworth Hall

If you were to search for Wingerworth Hall, you would only find two gate houses at the end of the old drive, the lake, the stables and two independent sections (the north and south blocks) because the magnificent hall was demolished in the 1920s.

Back in 1551, Nicholas Hunloke purchased the Manor of Wingerworth from the Curzons and it remained the Hunloke family seat until 1920. The inventory of an early Wingerworth Hall is housed at the Lichfield Record Office, but the only pictorial evidence is in a marquetry table now on display at the Victoria and Albert Museum in London.

The south block of Wingerworth Hall – note the orb on the left-hand side of the photograph.

To give some indication of the size of the hall, in 1662 householders were taxed on the number of hearths they had. Wingerworth Hall is recorded as having eight, but by 1670 the number had increased to fourteen due to the addition of the north and south blocks. Between 1726 and 1730 the 3rd Baronet, Sir Thomas Windsor Hunloke commissioned a very lavish new Hall while retaining the north and south blocks. The family fortunes fluctuated over the years then in May 1920, Wingerworth Hall and 260 acres of land were offered for sale.

Sadly there were no takers so the estate was divided up and a second auction was held in July 1920. The magnificent hall was purchased with demolition rights for £12,000. The north and south blocks were sold separately and transformed into five separate dwellings.

When North Side on the south block came up for sale I was very interested and went to look round. It was in a terrible state, but I could visualise it as a fantastic home so before returning the key I went back with my camera. I wandered from room to room breathing in the strange listening silence. Was it my imagination or was I being watched? Perhaps it was Ann Ash! I'd heard the story of this distant relative of the Hunlokes, who lived to be very old and senile. In her declining years she became convinced that the Hunlokes had stolen all her money and threatened to come back and haunt them. Supposedly she did. Before the main Hall was pulled down she was regularly seen at an attic window and walking along the top corridor. Her grave is in the churchyard nearby and on her gravestone, although now indecipherable, is the following inscription:

Here lieth the body of Ann Ash who departed this life April 24th 1789, aged 104. Descended from a good family in London, yet by the vicissitudes of fortune, she would have felt all the miseries of penury and indigence, but for the benevolent assistance of distant relatives, who supported her for the last fifty years of her life. Reader, whoever thou art, reflect on the instability of human enjoyments, and while in they flower, extend that benevolence to thy fellow creatures, which thou in thy time mayest be necessitated to receive from the bounty of others.

It was several days later when I was looking at the photographs that I noticed strange green shapes, as dim as wood smoke. I showed them to my daughter who let out a gasp of disbelief. She could make out human features in the green blob, and I had missed the reflection of the face that peered from the bathroom mirror until she pointed it out. I showed the photographs to a psychic friend of mine.

'This is not the right house for you,' she said examining the prints. 'You would not be happy there. The spirits are not welcoming you. Stay away.'

I went back just once more to return the key through the letter box. I didn't go inside.

Mrs Evelyn Davis and three generations of her family have lived in the north block for over thirty years and have all experienced paranormal activity. The Hunlokes were staunch Roman Catholics who often worshipped in secret, and not only have the family discovered a priest hole, the ghost of a fully robed priest has also been seen wandering around the corridors. June saw a maid in full uniform leaning on her hands, looking pensively out of a window over the garden, and late one evening Mrs Davis heard someone drop a tray. Assuming it was her son, Alan, taking a snack to bed, she got up to reprimand him and clear up the mess, but there was no one around, no mess, and Alan was not even in the house. Could it have been the phantom maid?

Revolution House

This charming thatched cottage at Whittington, formerly known as the Cock and Pynot Inn (pynot is a Derbyshire term for a magpie), dates back to the seventeenth century when farmhouses also doubled as ale houses. What makes this one special is that on 2 June 1688, while on a hunt, four noblemen sought shelter here from a heavy storm. Two of them, William Cavendish, 4th Earl of Devonshire (great, great grandson of Bess of Hardwick) and Thomas Osbourne, Earl of Damby were

The bathroom at Wingerworth Hall, with the image in the mirror.

political enemies, but, together with John Darcy, grandson and heir of the Earl of Holderness, and Henry Booth, Baron Delamere, they agreed to settle their differences for the good of the country. They plotted to dethrone the Catholic King James II who had ascended to the throne on the death of his brother Charles II in 1685, and invite his nephew the Protestant Prince William of Orange, who also happened to be married to James' daughter Mary, to become King of England. Cavendish led the discussion sitting in a historic chair in what is now called the Plotting Parlour.

The plan worked and it became known as the Glorious Revolution as it was virtually bloodless. Prince William set sail for England and his boat anchored at Torbay on 5 November. He marched at the head of 13,000 men to Exeter, then on to London. On 23 December James escaped abroad and on 13 February 1689, his daughter Mary arrived from Holland to join her husband Prince William. Together they were proclaimed King and Queen of Great Britain and Ireland.

For his part in the plot, in 1694 William Cavendish was given the title of 1st Duke of Devonshire and the Cock and Pynot became known as Revolution House. The original chair is now on view in Hardwick Hall, but there is a copy at the Cock and Pynot.

It remained an ale house for the next century, but 200 years after the revolution it was in a poor state of repair. In 1938 it was taken over by the borough council and is now part of the Chesterfield Museum. Furnished as it would have been in those far off days, it has retained its charm, but it has also retained its ghosts.

Many people have sensed a presence in the building although they stress it is not threatening. Some have seen a face peering through the small, lead-paned windows. One lady looking out of the window felt a tug on her cardigan as if it was being pulled by a demanding child. She turned but she was alone. Others have seen a dog wandering through the room and some have felt it brush past their legs, but all agree that the atmosphere at Revolution House is calm and welcoming.

The Revolution House, Whittington.

On the anniversary of that historical meeting, there is commemorative rejoicing, and on 2 June 1988, Prince Charles joined 2,000 people and the descendents of the four plotters to celebrate the Glorious Revolution which took place 300 years before.

Hospital ghosts

Hospitals seem to have their fair share of ghostly spirits. Many Derbyshire hospitals were originally workhouses, so it is inevitable that such buildings have a highly charged emotional atmosphere, and have inherited a permanent reminder of the suffering and death of many people. It is therefore not surprising that hospital staff and former patients should have experienced images of past events. Many accounts are uncannily similar and as some of these Derbyshire properties are still in use, the stories are generalised to conceal their identity for the peace of mind of new patients, because some paranormal activity is still being experienced to this day.

Inexplicably blocked doorways are a regular occurrence. There are doors that seem unaccountably stuck then are suddenly free, and fire escape doors that burst open of their own accord. There are visitors that step into lifts and vanish, patients that shouldn't be there, and staff from another time and era who seem to be hard at work.

Porters and members of staff regularly report trolleys being pushed by unseen hands, and hearing the distinct sound of footsteps ascending or descending spooky stairwells and walking along creepy corridors. After the death of one patient, for quite a lengthy period the familiar and distinctive pattern of his footsteps was frequently heard shuffling around his former ward.

Many nurses have sensed strange atmospheres and there are numerous reports of bizarre happenings on wards. A former nurse recalls how, at around 4.30 a.m. one morning, the sound of voices brought two members of staff out of the ward office to investigate. The talking was coming from the end bed where, to their disbelief, hung a misty cloud. Although no doors or windows were open, as they approached the mist quickly disappeared and the nurses found that the patient was dead. It is believed by some that in our dying moments consciousness begins to drift to a higher level of existence. The person then passes out of the physical body and into the etheric body. This process is sometimes

Left: *Florence Nightingale, Derbyshire's most famous nurse. Her statue is above the door of the Nightingale Nursing Home, Derby.* Right: *The Royal Infirmary, Derby.*

witnessed as a silver thread or mist rising from the physical body. The spirit will then linger by the body for a short while before casting off the etheric body and moving into the spirit world.

On another occasion, a nurse reporting for duty noticed a naval officer sitting beside one of the beds. He gave her a sad smile and although it was well past visiting hours, the nurse didn't bother him as the patient was very ill and not expected to live through the night. Returning the visitor's sad smile she carried on with her duties. She went to check on the patient a little while later and found his condition had deteriorated further. As there was no sign of the visitor, she asked her companion where he had gone. The girl replied that she had not seen anyone since they had come on duty. At about 2 a.m. the nurse noticed the visitor again and she realised that the uniform with its tasselled epaulettes was not of this era. She walked towards him, but the figure melted away as she approached. Later that night, the patient died.

While sitting at her desk, a nurse on night duty caught sight of an elderly female patient walking down the ward. Thinking that she was confused and wandering, the nurse went to escort her back to bed, but as she approached, the woman just disappeared. Another nurse saw a patient near the far end of the ward pulling on a dressing gown. She walked briskly over to see why the patient was out of bed, but the figure just vanished.

One nurse described a night when the sound of running water was suddenly heard. On investigating, a sluice room was found to be the source with its taps fully on although no one had used the room that evening. Having turned off the water, the nurse reported to the sister who simply smiled and said, 'Oh it sounds as if she's up to her old tricks again.' Apparently, a former nurse committed suicide after the death of a child in her care and her ghost now returns to turn on the taps and occasionally turn off the oxygen supply.

There are reports of other former nurses returning to check on their patients. One, described as a golden-haired girl is regularly reported leaning over a particular bed, and three young men who were convalescing watched a nurse in a long grey dress as she drifted between the beds then walked right through the fireplace.

A porter at one of the hospitals was about to take someone into the morgue to identify a dead relative, but decided to check the corpse first. He walked into the morgue and was amazed to see a young man sitting on one of the two trolleys. 'What are you doing in here?' he asked in astonishment. The man just grinned then appeared to float away from the trolley and straight through a wall. The porter resigned his job immediately as he could never face entering the mortuary again.

Many of the old hospitals with their grim Victorian façades are now largely disused. Although some like the old Royal Hospital at Chesterfield find a new lease of life as the headquarters of a car-hire company many, like Grove Hospital in Shardlow have to face the bulldozers.

Grove Hospital

Apparently, a number of ex-patients of the former Grove Hospital in Shardlow, South Derbyshire, appear to be demonstrating from beyond the grave.

Workmen on the site claim to have seen ghostly figures flitting through former wards, felt icy blasts and heard strange bangs. Demolition expert Phil Massie, site manager for Carwarden Demolition of Ockbrook, Derby, feels that the supernatural goings on must be because ex-patients did not want the hospital to be knocked down; so are the demolition team facing a protest with a difference?

At first the men ignored the inexplicable bangings, the grey mist that covered part of the building and the icy blasts that gusted from nowhere.

'I am not a great believer in this kind of thing, but there is definitely something that is not quite right,' said Phil. 'The more work we do, the more things seem to happen. Some of the lads saw what they thought was someone walking past and concerned for the safety of a member of the public, shouted out a warning. They went to check where the person had gone, but there was no one there.'

The building was last inhabited by patients in December 2005, but it would seem that some are still residing there. In 2006, a group of ghost hunters did a nightly vigil in the empty shell of the ex-hospital and captured a number of orbs on camera.

Some orbs were floating down the empty corridors; others hovered over seating, particularly in one of the former day-rooms. Members of the group made spirit contact with a lady called Elsie or Goldie. She was sitting in a chair watching with interest what was going on. The group recorded similar experiences to those experienced by the workmen, and local psychic Jason Daine who was called in to investigate. He claimed that he was able to talk to a number of disgruntled and bemused ex-patients:

> These people are between our world and the next. I was speaking to a man called Henry who was being sick in a sink in one room. Then a lady called Claire told me she was born in Derby and she was taken to hospital because she was too ill to be left on her own. There is certainly plenty of activity here.

Grove Hospital was in the grounds of the former Shardlow Workhouse which was erected in 1816 and required Parliamentary approval in the form of the Shardlow and Wilne Poor Relief Act. The building was enlarged in 1838-39 to increase its capacity to house 230 inmates. A major redevelopment was carried out around 1899 and new buildings erected with a separate hospital block to the south east of the workhouse. Following reconstruction work, this re-opened in 1970 as Grove Hospital and was used to care for elderly patients recuperating after treatment elsewhere. It closed in December 2005 with its patients transferred to a new £15 million building at Derby's Royal Infirmary. In 2006, developers Miller Homes bought the site from Derby hospitals NHS Foundation Trust for more than £2.5 million and permission has been granted to build fifty-nine houses on the land, but will the former residents approve?

Two

GHOSTS OF THE UNDERGROUND

Derbyshire has always been a county rich in natural resources. Underneath the sculptured hills and valleys lie a honeycomb of caves, tunnels and long disused mines, many of which are said to be inhabited by the phantoms of yesteryear. In the light of day it is easy to offer explanations for weird events, but in the dark depths of the caves, caverns, mines and tunnels of Derbyshire, the imagination can run riot.

Cresswell Crags

Prehistoric man lived at Cresswell Crags situated on the Nottinghamshire/Derbyshire border. These cave dwellers would have shared their environment with a great variety of animals, some known to us today, some extinct for many years – woolly rhinoceros, woolly mammoth, cave bear, hyena, wolf, wild horse, bison, reindeer, lynx, wolverine and cave lion. Remains of these and Palaeolithic man have been found here, so it's not surprising to find that ghosts are said to be numerous too.

In the 1920s a Mr Lawson and his companion saw the figure of a stone-age man wearing what they described as a facial mask. This might sound strange until you consider that one of the greatest finds made in the 1930s in the cave known as Pin Hole, was a fine example of caveman art – an engraving on reindeer bone of a figure who appears to be dancing, and he is wearing a mask.

Others have seen the ghost of a caveman dressed in furs and skins standing in the entrance to several of the caves. In the 1950s, three youths were exploring the caves when by the light of their torches they saw what they described as a caveman squatting on the ground. Keeping their torches firmly fixed on him, they advanced towards him, but he simply disappeared.

In the 1980s, a couple were driving home after an evening out and halted at temporary traffic lights serving road works near the visitors centre at Cresswell Crags. The driver had his window down as it was a warm, summer evening when suddenly they felt an unexpected chill. He wound the window up. His wife, who was the passenger, looked out of the window. The sides of the road were uncultivated, the briars and bushes grew densely and almost touched the side of the car, then, less than 2ft away she noticed a pale, blurred, circular shape which appeared to be suspended or caught in a bush. She strained her eyes to see more clearly as the shape seemed to move backwards and forwards. She couldn't make out what it was but didn't discount the possibility of it being a practical joke played by someone hiding in the bushes.

As she stared hard at it, it became clearer and seemed to assume the features of an old woman with hollow cheeks, dark eyes, beaked nose and long dark hair. She later described it as a witch, or at least the stereotype image of a witch with warts and all, but it was the piercing hateful eyes that seemed to stare right through her that finally convinced her that this was something paranormal. When the fully formed face with no attached body began to float towards the car, the woman screamed in terror. Her husband took one look at the eerie face, slammed the car in gear and shot off.

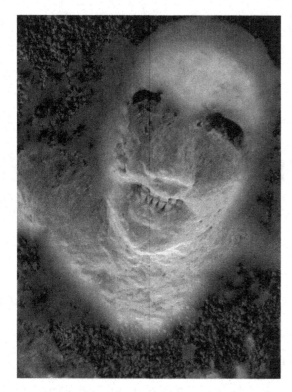

When the fully formed face with no attached body began to float towards the car, the woman screamed in terror.

The woman was so shocked by the incident a doctor had to be called and he persuaded them to call the police, convinced that a stupid, potentially dangerous prank had been played on the lonely country lane.

The police searched the area but were unable to find any clue as to what could have been responsible for the incident. They even tried to enter the thick brambles and thorn bushes, but found it impossible. But this was not a solo incident. Around dawn a lorry driver was forced to brake hard and swerve to avoid a mysterious dark figure which appeared from the visitors centre side of Cresswell Crags and crossed the road where it disappeared. Thoroughly shaken by his experience, he later described the figure as female and floating and seemingly headless.

Thor's Cave

On the opposite side of the county, located in the Manifold Valley not far from Wetton Village is Thor's Cave, a natural antediluvian cave that gets its name from the Norse god of Thunder who was the son of Woden. When excavation took place in 1864 an upright skeleton was found dating from the Neolithic age.

Like many such caves, ancient man regarded this as an entrance to a world of the supernatural, which could be why tales circulate that it is guarded by the phantom of a Roman soldier. More recently is has been chosen for the filming of such horror cult classics as *The Lair of the White Worm*.

The caves around Matlock Bath are said to be used by practicing witches and Derbyshire's allegedly oldest witchcraft coven 'The Coven of the Ram' is still said to practice their ancient religion in one of the caves here. Another cave in this area is said to be haunted by a legion of Roman soldiers.

The view from the mouth of Thor's Cave.

Poole's Cavern

Like many of Derbyshire's natural caves, Poole's cavern at Buxton was formed by the action of rainwater percolating through cracks and joints in the limestone rocks over many thousands of years. The scouring action of the sand and rocks carried in the waters assisted the enlargement of the cave which was believed to be inhabited by Neolithic man. The interior of the cave is a constant 45 degrees Fahrenheit and the River Wye running through the cave would have provided fresh water. There have been many archaeological finds such as bones, flints, pottery, coins, silver ingots, globules of bronze, and jewellery which would indicate that as well as being a dwelling place, Poole's Cavern was also used as a burial ground.

The cave gets its name from a highwayman named Poole who lived in the cave during the fourteenth and fifteenth centuries. According to some theories Poole was not a villain but a political refugee and member of an aristocratic family who resided at Poole Hall in Staffordshire. Because of his strong political views he was forced to leave his comfortable abode and live in the cave. Whether he lived in the cavern or not, local legend says that this is where he hid his treasure, much of which has never been found.

The shadowy figure of Poole is still purportedly seen searching for this lost treasure deep within the cave, and in the Poached Egg Chamber, one formation resembles an enormous cat and legend has it that this is Poole's petrified cat waiting for him to return.

In August 1997, a couple visiting Poole's Cavern reported a buzzing sound in the air around the entrance. They spent some time trying to locate a large nest of wasps which they assumed was causing the noise, but failed to find anything. These kinds of noises are often associated with rocks reacting under pressure and can also manifest in bizarre thuds and reverberations. There is a close correlation between the noises, glowing lights and other paranormal phenomena that are said to haunt the area.

The Devil's Bolt Hole

It was believed that dark forces lived at the bottom of a deep pot hole a mile north of the village of Peak Forest. It was given the name The Devil's Bolt Hole as it was once thought to be bottomless, the entrance to hell and a refuge for the Devil.

In the fifteenth century, a man called Charles Cotton was supposedly lowered down on a one mile long length of rope and still didn't reach the bottom. In the sixteenth century, the Earl of Leicester conducted an experiment. A suitably reimbursed Elizabethan peasant was lowered down into the dangerous chasm and reached 750ft. When he was hauled up, he was said to have an expression of sheer terror on his face, and was ranting and raving like a mad man. He never recovered and died later that day. From this, the Earl deduced that the hole was a direct link to hell and the dead man must have come face to face with the Devil.

An equally unorthodox experiment was conducted by two ruffians who forced a man to stand on the edge of the hole then step over the edge. They claimed to have heard the crackle of flames as he dropped into the arms of Satan.

There is one tale of an old woman's goose that flew down the hole and after being given up for lost, emerged at the mouth of the Peak Cavern at Castleton, over two miles away. This might seem rather far-fetched yet it is given credence because in limestone country streams can disappear underground to reappear elsewhere.

Eighteenth-century investigations said it was 600yds deep, but the sides actually drop 186ft plus a further 75ft into a vast stalactitic cavern. It is 110ft by 20ft wide at the surface. A cavern like this with a vertical pitch is in fact a pot hole and this is the only true pot hole in the Peak District. The Devil's Bolt Hole had such a macabre reputation that it was given a change of name. It became known as Eldon Hole which is probably derived from Elfdom Hole, so from allegedly being the abode of the Devil it was changed to that of fairies and other supernatural beings.

Castleton Caverns

The Castleton Caverns are a mixture of natural caverns, early tunnelling accomplished with sheer muscle power, and modern innovation to produce show caverns that attract thousands of visitors annually.

Speedwell Cavern at the foot of Winnats Pass took its name from the Speedwell Tavern, the public house which is now the gift shop standing just outside the cavern entrance. Visiting Speedwell Cavern is a memorable and dramatic experience as the subterranean canal excavated by lead miners in the 1770s is navigated by boat.

The legend of the Fiery Drake is told around Castleton. The Fiery Drake is a floating ball of orange fire that is said to drift along the underground shafts. The old miners associated its appearance with disaster.

Treak Cliff Hill is situated on the north side of Winnats Pass and within the hill are two well-known caves, Treak Cliff Cavern which is probably the most attractive, and Blue John Cavern, in which is the famous Blue John Mine. In these mines, numerous people have seen the ghost of an old man dressed in grey who suddenly disappears. People have experienced being touched or spoken to by disembodied voices of long-dead miners who simply can't rest, and the ghost of the Blue John Mine is said to announce his presence by whistling.

*The subterranean canal
at Speedwell Cavern.*

The Devil's Arse

The Devil's Arse is the name given to the largest natural cave-entrance in the British Isles and is where the Devil disappeared after being defeated by the power of good. With its dripping wells, underground rivers and other mysteries including the Devil's Cellar, a more desirable residence for Old Nick is hard to imagine. It's even apparent as you approach the cavern and walk beside the brook which comes from deep inside the cave. On occasions, this brook becomes an angry, yellow, opaque torrent. 'That,' say the locals, 'Is when the Devil is relieving himself.'

But despite its link with the Devil, this cave is actually called Peak Cavern. It has also been known as the High Peak House of Labour because in previous centuries it actually housed a small subterranean community of up to thirty rope makers and their families. Traces of their sunless, stone-built, thatched cottages plus stables and an inn can still be seen on the cave walls to the right, and the soot from their chimneys is still visible on the roof of the cavern. An engraving dated 1721 shows the cottages which stood for a further hundred years or so.

Each master had his walk, and seven rope walks traverse the stupendous excavation. They say the rope makers didn't pay a rent and got most commodities free because it was believed that anyone who took money from them would finish up hanging from one of their hang-man's ropes. Their other products were window sashes, ropes for industry and shipping, bell and tow ropes. Another custom which was upheld until 1969 was to present every Castleton bride with a Peak Cavern clothes line.

The last person to live in Peak Cavern was Mary Knight who died in 1845, but the rope making continued until 1974 when the last rope maker Mr Bert Marrison retired at the age of eighty-nine. It is still possible to see the weird, gallows-like uprights and posts, with flying ropes and hanging weights, with adjacent suggestions of vast wheels and curious figures standing out against the darkness. It's also possible to imagine the ghosts of those rope makers are still hard at work.

Haunted mines

First the lead, then the coal miners burrowed their way in the dark underground mines which like the caves and caverns in Derbyshire are now purportedly haunted by eerie, mystical presences. Many of these tales were passed verbally so it is not surprising to find that ghost stories and tales of strange sightings were rife amongst the mining communities. Most were handed down through the generations of miners by word of mouth, but occasionally something is found on paper, like this poem by Henry Walker:

> From flickering tallow candle, the lead-miner flicks the thief
> To rid the spirit splutter in his quaint and crude belief
> Then turning quickly, down the vein he sees a pale light shine
> His heart beats fast. Is it the spectre of the mine?
> Along the silent gallery, gripping his candle tight
> Swiftly the miner followed but as quickly sped the light
> Till at the limit of the vein it vanished without sign
> The miner's blood turned cold. It was the spectre of the mine.
> A sudden crash and fall of rocks; the miner met his doom
> The shining ore he vainly sought now glistened on his tomb.
> In lead-miners law is written, let those who can define
> Why none may live that look upon the Spectre of the Mine

A medieval carving of a lead miner – the T'Owd Man in Wirksworth Church.

Lead was certainly mined in Derbyshire before the arrival of the Romans in AD 45. Stimulated by the demand during the sixteenth and seventeenth centuries, lead mining expanded to become a major industry in the limestone country of Derbyshire which extends roughly from Castleton in the north to Wirksworth in the south, Buxton in the west and Matlock in the east.

T'Owd man was a strange figment of Peak District lead-mining lore, his domain the dark and dangerous subterranean world of the miners, and abandoned workings in particular. Lead miners looked on T'Owd Man as the collective spirit of both their own predecessors and of the very mines themselves. T'Owd man was offered great respect. The miners customarily left him their best piece of ore set with a burning candle before leaving the mine on Christmas Eve.

In Wirksworth church a quaint stone carving of a lead miner has been nicknamed T'Owd Man, whereas Manlove's chronicles of 1653 used the term in reference to disused workings.

No miner ought of an Old Man to set,
To seek a lead-mine or lead oar to get,
Until the Barghmaster a view hath taken
And find such work an old work quite forsaken.

A drawing of the Smelting House in Middleton Dale by Francis L. Chantrey, 1817.

The headless ghost of Wenley Hill

A miner was excavating fluorspar at a mineral outcrop at Wenley Hill, Youlgreave. It was a lonely job so when one day he encountered an old man in the lane, the miner invited him to join him while he worked.

'Where are you working?' asked the old man.

'Wenley Hill,' said the miner.

'Not likely lad. Ah'm not coming up theer. It's haunted.'

The miner laughed and tried to assure the old man that it was not. But the old man insisted he knew of the appearance of a headless dog, sinister influences and uncanny happenings. He also pointed out the uncanny stillness and lack of bird song in the area, then, to back this up, he told the miner a story. One day, he and his brother had been walking along Wenley Hill to attend to some cattle at farm buildings in the corner of a nearby field. As they walked, the figure of a man appeared and preceded them along the lane. Then just as suddenly, he disappeared. Both men had witnessed this and also, more surprisingly, they both agreed that the man was headless.

Superstitious miners

For centuries, dowsing rods were used to find ore and many miners were under the naïve belief that it grew in the underground veins. Whistling in a mine was banned as the sound was believed to drive the ore away. When a pumping engine at Calver didn't work properly, the miners laid rowan branches on it hoping to counteract the witchcraft which they believed had stopped it functioning.

Miners, like many others who work in hazardous occupations were greatly influenced by superstition, believing these to be signals from God that should be heeded. On their way to work they believed that seeing certain animals had significance. To see a rabbit was said to indicate an accident pending. When a large black dog crossed the path of a Bradwell miner, he considered it an omen and would not go down the mine, but the colleague who was with him insisted on work as usual and was killed when the roof fell in.

A drawing of a lead miner at work.

Early twentieth-century miners.

All mines were thought to be inhabited by a ghost or an elf who was held responsible for any casualties or unexplained incidents occurring in or around the mines. If a miner was overcome by choke-damp (carbon dioxide) he was brought to the surface where he would be laid face down in soil where a patch of turf had been removed. Derbyshire lead miners believed in the Knockers whose hammers could be heard tapping deep in the workings. In Bradwell, when the miners went home on Christmas Eve they left half a candle burning, and many offerings were left in the old workings to placate T'Owd Man. These included tiny clay pipes known as fairy pipes and children's shoes.

The ghost of the Magpie Mine

Evidence of lead mining is spread all over the Peak District, but one of the best preserved lead mines whose surface works have been restored as a visitor attraction is the Magpie Mine which stands on the hills above the village of Sheldon near Bakewell. It was worked for over 300 years, but had a rather troubled past. Is that surprising with a name like magpie (traditionally a bird of ill omen associated with witchcraft)?

Lead miners were generally pugnacious and would fight bitterly for their rights, so when, in 1824, tunnels from the Magpie Mine and the adjacent Red Soil Mine ran close together and merged, disputes over the lead-bearing veins were inevitable. These lasted for several years during which time there was fighting and vandalism, then tragedy occurred when the miners tried to smoke each other out. Three miners died of asphyxiation in 1833 and it is said that their widows put a curse on the mine. Since that time, there has been a history of floods, fires, hauntings and roof-falls.

Eventually, flooding caused its closure in 1926, but it was said that if you stood at the top of the old shaft, you could hear the ghostly voices of the long-dead miners calling in the galleries below.

In 1946, a party of speleologists were exploring the Magpie Mine when one of them saw a man with a candle walking along the tunnel before suddenly disappearing. A photograph of another member of the party on a raft in a flooded tunnel at the mine showed a second man standing apparently on 9ft of water. Even though it is no longer worked, could it be that the old miners still frequent the Magpie Mine?

Magpie Mine.

Mystical mines

Nellie Kirkham, an authority on Derbyshire lead mines tells of a ghost that haunts Hanging Flatt Mine near Eyam. He has been seen underground and on the surface carrying a spade over his shoulder. He wanders along the old workings muttering to himself and oblivious to onlookers. A lady who lived at a farm close to the mine said that she had heard the strokes of a pick within the closed mine.

Two miners walking along the drift heard footsteps in the darkness behind them and believing it to be a colleague, turned to wait for his approach. As they did so, the footsteps ceased and there was no one present.

Many mines are haunted by strange, eerie noises that escape from the rocks, but at Eyam they have a story to explain these. Two young women arrived in Eyam without a penny and without wishing to besmirch their reputations, lived at the camp set up by the lead miners. One day a lamp was overturned causing a fire in the hut which was over the entrance to the mine shaft. This badly burnt one woman and trapped the other. People shouted to tell her to go down the shaft until the fire was put out, but in her panic she tripped, fell down the shaft and was killed. It is said that now her ghost is heard screeching in agony.

Sallet Hole Mine is said to be haunted by the ghost of an old man wearing a cap and long coat. He is accompanied by a ghostly dog and both are said to disappear when approached. Black dogs are said to dwell in mines and caves and are often seen only as fire-coloured eyes with a dark, ominous shape behind them.

Coombs Dale, near Stoney Middleton is dotted with old mine workings, but watch out for other dangers too. At the end of Coombs Dale is a gate known as Black Harry Gate, named after a highwayman who in the early eighteenth century frequently attacked and robbed the packhorse trains that crossed the moors in that area. On a dark, windy night it's easy to imagine he's still there.

The Goodluck Mine was sunk sometime in the eighteenth century high in the hills above Via Gellia by men in search of lead. Some time later in that century, probably in the 1790s, a miner hanged himself there, but the Barmote Court compassionately recorded the death as an accident to save his family the shame of a verdict of suicide. The ghost of that man Gamaliel Hall is now thought to haunt the mine. Since those early days the mine has been enlarged and an adit was pushed through in 1830. In 1831 the miners had reached a point where they recorded their initials and the date on the cheek of the vein. Amongst those initials is a descendant of Gamaliel Hall, also called Gamaliel.

The mine was deepened further and many veins of lead worked until in 1953 it was declared no longer profitable and was closed leaving the ghost of Gamaliel Hall in peace to wander its many passages.

In 1972, a small group of enthusiasts dug their way into the mine and over the years lovingly restored it. Recently the Goodluck Mine Preservation Club was formed to preserve and open the mine.

KAPS Paranormal based in Sheffield visited in June. They offer haunted night trips to those who are looking for an experience out of the ordinary. The group was satisfied that both within the mine and in the coe, the miners shelter on the surface, enough odd and out-of-the-ordinary sensations were felt to confirm the belief that someone or something had left a presence in there. They intend to visit again with more sophisticated equipment to check it out. Their website can be found at www.kapsparanormal.co.uk

Was it an uncapped mine?

It wasn't just underground where the dangers were ever present; in lead mining areas uncapped mines were a constant danger for animals and people as this story shows. Dorothy Mately had the rather unsavoury reputation of swearing, cursing, lying and thieving, but when accused of these indiscretions she always protested her innocence and had the habit of looking perplexed and hurt, and uttering the words 'If this be so, may the ground swallow me up!' One day it actually did.

Dorothy was employed along with other local women and small boys on the surface of a lead mine on the outskirts of Ashover. Every day she washed away the spoil from the ore as it was brought up from the mine. One particular day, a boy had taken off his breeches and laid them aside and was working in his drawers. When he checked in his breeches pocket, he found that the two pennies were missing. He accused Dorothy of stealing them but she hotly denied it and protested her innocence by stating, 'If I did, may God make the earth open up and swallow me.'

George Hodgkinson, an Ashover man was standing nearby as Dorothy was swearing her innocence, but he'd heard it all before and turned away in disgust. He'd hardly gone 10yds when he heard a scream, and turning round, he saw Dorothy spin round before disappearing into a large crater that had suddenly opened up on the hillside. She sank about three yards then came to rest on a ledge. Her screams for help brought an immediate response from those present yet before they could organise to pull her out, a large stone from the side fell on her head, breaking her skull. Immediately more earth fell over and around her, covering her completely. She was eventually dug out and in her pocket was found just two pennies.

In the parish register, it is recorded: 'March 23rd 1660 Dorothy Mately, common law wife of John Flint of this parish, foreswore herself whereupon the ground opened and she sank over her head. Being found dead, she was buried March 25th'. Ashover was once a very profitable lead mining area and the ground would have a number of capped mine-shafts, but the likelihood of one suddenly opening up at that very moment was highly suspect; most people believe that Dorothy's tragic end came through divine intervention.

Matlock Mining Museum

In the Spring of 2007, a team from Living TV's *Most Haunted* series filmed at Matlock Mining Museum, which is housed in the Pavilion at Matlock Bath. As could be expected they unearthed some amazing details. In the ground floor museum area, footsteps and bangs are heard regularly and the team experienced a feeling of unease that couldn't be explained. They witnessed some rubbish in the corner move, and a light bulb exploded near them. David Wells the medium felt that a lot of the activity was caused by a miner. He was able to communicate with him and learnt that his name is something beginning with the letter 'T', possibly Tom. He died aged thirty-six or thirty-seven, crushed to death, probably in the mine.

The obvious question was then asked – why does Tom haunt the Pavilion? There isn't and never was a mine there, but according to David Wells, Tom appears to be looking for something. The museum is full of mining artefacts, so is he looking for something that once belonged to him? Is he looking for his tools? Is that why he haunts the place? Most of the tools on display were found in disused mines, so had Tom's tools been buried when he met his untimely death?

Tom is not alone in the museum and pump room. There is another man called Robert. He's a sinister presence and responsible for the banging and whistling that is regularly heard. The presence of both these men is obvious from the smell of body odour and the sound of heavy wheezing which was picked up very clearly by the sound equipment. It couldn't be explained away, so Yvette Fielding the presenter asked, 'Was that you Robert?' She received two taps in response.

On the first floor there is a strong male presence and cold spots on the upstairs corridor. Machinery noises have been reported. Footsteps are heard that sound like shoes on concrete yet the floors are carpeted. On the upper floor of the Dome, someone threw something, a typical form of poltergeist activity. The trap-door stuck. They couldn't open it but could feel some form of vibration as they tried. The place went very cold and they had to telephone for help to get out. All the crew involved agreed that the place is alive with activity.

Matlock Mining Museum, alive with activity.

Coal-mining

Just like the ghostly tales that circulated amongst the lead miners, the coal miners also had a rich store of paranormal tales. There are classic ghost examples, like the story of the lone compressor attendant who spoke to a miner who then simply disappeared, or the two colliery officials who saw a man enter a part of a mine where no one else was, and a search found no trace of the man.

A collier working alone deep below the ground at Bolsover colliery was approached by another miner who asked the way to the pit shaft. He then watched in amazement as the stranger walked straight through the closed cage doors and vanished. Later the collier was to describe the man as dressed in very old-style working clothes, with a candle burning on the front of his hat. Many nineteenth- and twentieth-century miners wore the Bradder Bowler made at Bradder aka Bradwell, attaching a candle to the front rim by means of a lump of clay.

Production at Shirebrook Colliery was severely disrupted by a report in the *Star* evening paper during November 1958. The report told how John McGoary, an Irish navvy, was working deep underground at Shirebrook colliery when he saw a man holding a light, walk past him. He recognised the man as Wilfred Hales. Another miner, Keith Plant, verified this, as he too had seen Wilfred Hales. The problem was, Wilfred Hales, a fellow collier aged thirty, had collapsed and died in January 1955. The haunting caused temporary unrest amongst the workforce, and management blamed the ghost for low productivity.

Barry Jones left Cotgrave Pit soon after witnessing an incident in 1984. He was a quarter of a mile underground when he saw a man dressed in overalls and a pit helmet walk through a concrete wall. Barry is not the only one to see the ghost of this miner who haunts Cotgrave Pit. Three years later, nineteen-year-old Gary Pine encountered the same ghost and once again it disappeared by walking into a solid pit wall. In a state of shock, Gary had to be taken to the surface on a stretcher. After a haulage truck accident in 1979, several miners refused to work at that location as it was thought that the same ghost may have been responsible.

A spectral miner called 'Flatcap' roams the gates and workings at Silverhill Colliery. Apparently one day he approached the deputy and complained that his snap-tin had gone back up in the cage

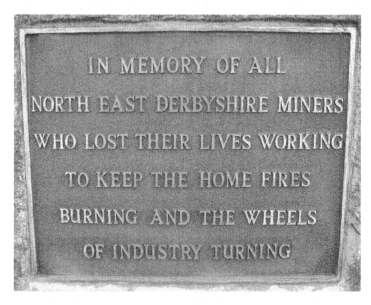

A plaque commemorating the Derbyshire miners.

43

Left: *Coal tubs, originally pulled by pit ponies are now used for decorative purposes at Clay Cross.*

Below: *The winding wheel, now just a reminder of the vast mining industry of north east Derbyshire, stands alongside a dedication plaque at Clay Cross.*

by mistake. The deputy assured him that he'd telephone the surface and get it sent back before the man's dinner break, then realised he was talking to thin air.

In the early days of mining, pit ponies played a valuable role in transporting the coal along the underground passages. Most of these ponies never saw the light of day as they were stabled in underground stalls and cared for by an ostler who fed and watered then and generally took care of them after the shifts were over. For many years Markham's ostler was a man called Archie who after many years of service died suddenly in the stables. Shortly after Archie's death, Ron Webster was underground in an area near the stables. He glanced across at the ponies and in the dim light saw someone feeding them. Looking closer he realised that it was Archie who had come back in spirit to care for his ponies.

One of the ten shafts that mark the line of the Clay Cross tunnel.

Markham colliery is also haunted by the ghost of a deputy. He was always seen in a part of the mine that regularly flooded and many of the men refused to venture into that area alone. Drainage pumps were installed to solve the problem and these had to be activated at regular intervals. The men that carried out this task often reported the phantom deputy standing in a corner watching them work.

Clay Cross Tunnel

Victorian railway engineers are remembered for their ability to produce long railway tunnels, and some of the longest are those that carry the railways through Derbyshire. The construction of these often required considerable effort, ingenuity and dogged determination.

In 1835 George Stephenson surveyed the route for the North Midland Railway Co.'s line between Derby and Leeds. Seven tunnels were needed, and the longest was to be under what was then the rural community of Clay Cross.

Excavating began in February 1837 from both tunnel entrances and from ten shafts. The bore was driven through shale and extensive seams of coal, so in order to mine these minerals the enterprising George formed his own company which became the Clay Cross Co. The tunnel, 1 mile 24yds long (1.6km) was completed in 1840, but accidents had been frequent and it is thought that eleven men were killed during construction.

Is it the ghost of these men that have been seen walking through the tunnel holding their flickering candles, or could it be the great George Stephenson himself?

Three

PUBS WITH WHINES & GHOSTLY SPIRITS

Ghost stories and pubs seem to go together like gin and tonic, so if you fancy a pub-crawl with a difference, take a look at a selection of our county's haunted pubs that have baffled investigators and terrified landlords, cleaners and customers for generations.

The Boat Inn

When Bill Gates, a previous landlord of the Boat Inn, Cromford, changed the beer cellar into another bar/function room, he acquired more than he bargained for. The builders knocked away an old fireplace with bread ovens, and behind this found a room that stretched under the road to Scathin. The room was empty, but that night, Bill was woken by noises coming from the cellar area.

Glasses were being smashed and a sound like the crash of a pile of beer trays had to be investigated, but when Bill crept downstairs expecting to see total destruction, he found nothing. Bill was totally bewildered and pondered on how these noises could have been made, when the room did not even contain a bar. This noisy destruction continued for a week, then stopped. That's when the footsteps began.

These footsteps walking along the first floor still continue today according to Ken, the present landlord, but the scariest thing happened to Bill Gates' thirteen-year-old-son. Bill went out leaving his son alone in the pub, but to make sure he was safe, Bill locked all the outside doors. It wasn't long before the boy heard footsteps and he ran to hide in one of the downstairs rooms where he could lock the door securely from the inside (the room where the pool table now stands). The footsteps approached the door and he waited and watched in horror as the doorknob began to turn. When Bill returned, he found his son in a state of sheer terror.

Voices, materialisation and mischievous spirits are all active at the Boat Inn. There is also a sad story attached. Alice, a young girl was apparently kicked to death by horses in what was once the stable of the Boat Inn. It is believed her ghost still lingers here. She is said to be responsible for taps being turned on. She calls the names of people working in the bar, particularly the last there at night. Alex, one of the staff, has actually seen her. One day Alex was fooling about and locked Ken in the cellar. As he pocketed the key, Alex turned to see a little girl, about six years old, standing a short distance away. She was wearing a white dress with a broad sash and was scowling at him. She obviously didn't like Ken being locked in the cellar.

Numerous soldiers have also been seen, wearing uniforms ranging from the eighteenth to the twentieth century. After he left, Bill Gates kept in touch with the Revd Louds, who has now died, and he told him this story. The Royal Ancient Order of Buffalos had their meeting in the basement bar of the Boat Inn. One of their meetings was in progress when suddenly, without any warning, a lady in grey materialised, walked straight through the assembled group and disappeared through the far wall.

The Boat Inn, Cromford.

The Green Man and Black's Head Royal Hotel

The Green Man and Black's Head at Ashbourne is a mid-eighteenth-century inn with an unusual and rare 'gallows' sign which spans St John Street. It dates back to the busy coaching days when Ashbourne was the meeting point of six main coaching routes. The coach entrance to what were once the stables behind is now a covered courtyard, but the inn is perhaps now best known as the venue for the Shrovetide Football Game that takes place annually in the town.

It's a town centre pub with character and, according to the cleaner Doreen, a playful ghostly character too. She was cleaning one of the public bars when she saw a salt and pepper pot glide across a table by the window and stop just short of falling off the table top. She automatically reached over to put them back in the centre of the table and they immediately glided back again. She ran.

Doreen also told me about the scene when a guest staying in No. 2 bedroom had an unexpected service call. The lady, who was in bed at the time, heard a knock on the door and a maid entered. The guest watched in stunned silence as the maid walked across the room and disappeared through the wardrobe door.

Somerset House

Although now a pub, Somerset House, Calow, was formerly the house of a gentleman farmer who, like many others, participated in the rural pursuits of shooting and fishing.

The Green Man and Black's Head Royal Hotel, Ashbourne, with its rare 'gallows' sign.

However one day in 1934, a day's shooting was to end in tragedy when the ten-year-old son of the farm labourer who lived in the adjoining cottage picked up a gun to play with. Child-like he imitated the adults, aimed the gun at his seven-year-old sister and fired. His game had gone horribly wrong. The gun was loaded and the little girl died. She is buried in St Peter's churchyard, Calow.

Shortly afterwards, the building became a pub and subsequent landlords, customers and staff have experienced strange phenomena. On numerous occasions, customers have seen the apparition of a young girl and the description always tallies with that of the victim. One man was so sure it was a flesh and blood child, he at first thought it was his own daughter until he realised she was safely at home tucked up in bed.

Somerset House tenants firmly believe that this tragic little spectre is to blame for the strange occurrences that frequently happen. Items at the back of a shelf have fallen off without disturbing items in front of them. Doors will suddenly and unaccountably refuse to open. Lights will refuse to switch on or go off. On one occasion an electrician was called. He could find no reason for the problem, then suddenly they just began working normally again.

Staff hear their names being called by a mystery voice. In 1988 Carol the barmaid woke to find scratches on her arms. Claims that she could have scratched herself in her sleep were discounted because her nails were bitten short. Bill Davis the landlord, then pulled up his shirt to show similar scratches on his back. They too had appeared overnight and because of the angle, could not have been self-inflicted.

In 1990, Bill and Shirley had a visit from their son Peter and his five-year-old-son who live in London. The little boy got up in the night to go to the bathroom and saw the girl. He had been unafraid but asked who the girl was and why she had 'flown away'.

Somerset House.

The drunken miner and the ghost

The Ball Inn at Eyam was much frequented by the local miners and at the time of this story it was kept by a man called Stephen and his French-born wife Blandino, known to everyone as Blandy. She was an agreeable woman, but had perfected the art of mining the miners, plying them with drink for however long they had money in their pockets.

Tom Loxley, known to everyone as Cockeye, was a regular at the Ball Inn and although frequently worse for drink was always in good humour and popular with everyone. It was late one evening, his mates were ready to leave and they began to torment Cockeye, reminding him of the dark journey he faced alone past a lonely, ruined cottage that the locals said was haunted. They shunned it by day and night because in this crumbling, ivy-clad hovel they believed there lurked a malevolent ghost, dressed in a short bed-gown, a coarse woollen and cotton petticoat and a mob-cap, while on her feet she wore shoes with shining buckles. She was often seen on moonlit nights flitting across the valley at great speed. Strong doors and locks could not hold back this spirit who, like a cloud of smoke, was seen to enter nearby cottages through the keyhole or small holes in walls. Once inside she would tear bedclothes from the terrified occupants and torment them by pummelling and pinching their defenceless bodies.

'Come on Tom,' laughed Blandy. 'Take another drink to rally your spirits. Surely you are not afraid of a woman, dead or alive?'

The other miners laughed and Cockeye naturally rose to the bait and declared, 'No, nor the Devil himself. Pour me another drink Blandy.'

Stephen, the landlord, was not comfortable with such talk. He was firmly of the belief that if you call the Devil he will come in his own time, but Cockeye set off from the Ball Inn full of confidence and bravado vowing to face any ghost which might lurk in the lonely dell.

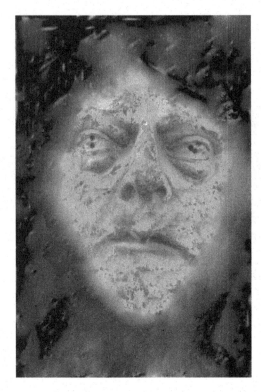

Did Cockeye encounter the ghost of the old woman on his lonely journey home?

As he approached the old ruined cottage, his courage began to ebb and his drunken imagination seemed to see in the shadows a twisted human form that moved and writhed towards him. He stood transfixed, too terrified to go on, too frightened to turn back in case the thing should rise up and pursue him. With a choking groan his legs gave way and he fell face down in the dirt. Shaking uncontrollably, he felt his ankles gripped by icy hands as he was dragged at a fast pace down the dell. As the grip tightened and the coldness increased, he fainted.

It was warmer, gentler hands which gripped and shook a sober Cockeye awake in the morning. Stephen, the pub landlord had found him half in and half out of the stream which winds through the dell. Its icy waters had nearly frozen him to death.

There were some that said that it was all conjured up by Cockeye's drink-sodden mind, that the icy grip of the ghost was the water of the stream he had fallen into, but no one could convince Cockeye of that. He stuck to his story for the rest of his life and never touched another alcoholic drink.

The Golden Fleece

This pub in the centre of Chesterfield is haunted by Cheeky Charlie, a mischievous rather than ancient or mysterious spirit. He is thought to be Charles White, an alderman of Chesterfield and landlord of one of the four pubs which once occupied the 75-yard strip between Knifesmithgate and High Street, now taken up by the Golden Fleece.

Helen Cooke wife of landlord Glyn will not remain alone in the upstairs rooms. The couple's dog howls and whines if anyone tries to force him upstairs. Charlie seems to be free to roam and spends a good deal of time in the bar and cellars. A previous landlord called in a medium who told him there were definitely ghosts there, and that they were friendly enough, but Charlie can create havoc when he is in the mood.

Staff have gone into the cellar to connect new CO_2 cylinders only to find the empty one reconnected a few minutes later. Gas and beer taps are turned on and off, bottles and cleaning equipment are moved and in one incident, a member of the bar staff watched in amazement as a glass flew through the air behind the bar, hitting the kitchen door, only to be found standing unbroken on the floor.

The Malt Shovel

In 1799, Humphrey Moore, a rich farmer who lived in The Monastery at Old Wilne was responsible for the building of the Malt Shovel (formerly the Malt House), including the bay and the manager's house.

There were three breweries in Shardlow at the time all brewing their own beer and extracting malt by boiling barley which was then fed to cattle. During construction, Moore found a tramp sleeping in the brewery and was so incensed, he supposedly threw the tramp into a beer vat and drowned him, or at least that's one story. Another says that an unknown worker at the malt house fell into a boiling vat and died a horrible death. Whichever version you prefer, the fact is, something haunts the cellars of the Malt House.

Just after Mr and Mrs Howard moved into the Malt Shovel, some alterations were being made and when plaster was removed, dry rot was found. The builder decided to leave the work while he sought expert advice, but next morning, all the bricks had been removed and stacked neatly to reveal a wooden archway of an older door. Some time after this, a boy, who had been working alone in the old loading bay (now used by furniture removers as a store), claimed he had been kicked down the stairs. Everyone laughed until the foreman entered the pub and ordered a double brandy – he had just been kicked down the stairs. Neither the foreman nor the lad ever went in there alone again.

The Malt Shovel by the side of the canal at Shardlow.

Left: *The ancient timbers of the Royal Oak were exposed during the restoration work in 1898, shortly after William Stones Brewery purchased it.* Right: *The Royal Oak today.*

The Royal Oak

The Royal Oak stands on the corner of Iron Gate in the area known as The Shambles, and according to a plaque outside, it was built in the twelfth century, is the oldest inn in Chesterfield, and one of the oldest in England. That is not strictly accurate. It may be one of the oldest buildings, but it was originally a small dwelling house and did not become licensed as an inn until 1772 when it was extended into two adjacent buildings to provide stabling and a brewhouse. A further extension of the property took place in the mid–nineteenth century when two butcher's shops were purchased by George and William Batteson, maltsters, who then owned the property. It is from this time that our story originates.

The Shambles is the name given to the area where animals were butchered, so unsurprisingly the buildings along either side of this narrow collection of streets were dwelling houses, abattoirs and butcher's shops. John Platts was one of the butchers who had a shop in The Shambles, and George Collis who worked as a servant to the Barnes family at Ashgate House had invested heavily in this joint business venture with Platts. The arrangement wasn't working, and on the chill winter evening of Sunday 7 December 1845, twenty-six-year-old George Collis met John Platts in the Old Angel Inn near the market place and informed him that he intended to withdraw his money and move to a new life in Manchester.

This obviously provoked an argument and later witnesses were to report seeing two men pushing a third who seemed heavily drunk and unsteady on his feet. This caused no undue alarm in a rough area renowned for its drunkenness and prostitution. The men went into John Platts' shop, next door to the Royal Oak, and locked the door after them.

Above: *The Shambles east to west passage, c. 1885.*

Right: *The Shambles today.*

People reported hearing blows, moaning and the sound of something heavy being dragged along the floor. People who banged on the door asking what was wrong were told by Platts that he had drunk too much and was sick, but would soon be better. A light burnt in the shop past midnight, but cloths covered the windows making it impossible to see inside. On Monday the shop stayed closed all day but that evening three men were seen carrying what looked like a sheep pack out of The Shambles. They crossed Low Pavement and into Bunting's Yard, now Falcon Yard.

When Collis's absence was noted, suspicion fell on John Platts but as no body was found, people believed that Collis must have gone to Manchester as he had planned. Then on 28 August 1846 men emptying the cesspit in Falcon Yard discovered Collis's decomposed body. Platts was brought to trial at Derby Crown Court in March 1847 charged with wilful murder. He was hanged on 1 April 1847.

When the butcher's moved from The Shambles into the newly constructed market hall over 100 years ago, the Shambles changed dramatically and the Royal Oak was extended into the two neighbouring butcher's shops. One of these was the infamous butcher's shop that had been rented by John Platts. After that, even people who have never heard about the events on that dreadful Sunday night started feeling a strange, uncomfortable atmosphere. A psychic saw the faint figure of a man wearing a black hat and coat, while managers and staff frequently have the feeling they are being stared at. There is one particular corner where people don't like to sit. There is no doorway to cause a draft, yet it has a coldness that can't be accounted for, an occurrence that is so common in haunted properties, it is usually referred to as a psychic breeze.

The Victorian maid at the Peacock

A barman at the Peacock in Bakewell went down to the cellar and, when he tried to return, found that the door had mysteriously jammed. He banged and shouted for help, but despite there being many people in the pub, no one could hear him. He tried his mobile phone, but could not get a signal. Eventually, he managed to climb up the barrel chute. As he walked in through the door, people looked at him in surprise and asked where he'd been. When he told his story, they went to check the cellar door and found it opened easily and there was no means of blocking or locking the door. At other times, staff have found the beer taps turned on or off in the cellar, and three men standing at the bar saw a ghostly figure in the doorway.

The old stables adjoining the Peacock have now been converted into holiday lets. In 2007, one group of guests staying there explained to staff that they hadn't locked the rooms because they had left the maid in there. The staff looked puzzled. There was definitely no maid that fitted the description of a lady wearing a long dark dress with a full white apron over.

Ringwood Hall

Ringwood Hall, Brimington was originally called Brimington Hall. Built early in the nineteenth century, it was once owned by the Markham family, prominent landowners and industrialists responsible for the formation of Markham Works in Chesterfield. Charles Markham married Rosa Paxton, granddaughter of Sir Joseph Paxton, the head gardener of Chatsworth who was also a great designer. Amongst his other notable successes was to design and build the Crystal Palace, which housed the 1851 Great Exhibition in London. Charles and Rosa Markham's youngest daughter was Violet Rosa Markham who was born at Ringwood Hall in 1872, and went on to give her name to the school in Chesterfield.

Now Ringwood Hall is a very smart hotel and leisure complex but the Markham family seem to have left their mark in more ways than one. Staff have seen vaporous figures walking along the corridors, and a few years ago, a security guard spotted a ghostly figure sitting in an armchair in the hall. The manager was a disbeliever until he witnessed a ghostly glow around a portrait of the late Vanessa Markham. It seems therefore that there are a few spirits around that are not of the liquid variety.

The Derwent Water Arms

Many years ago, a landlord of the Derwent Water Arms in Calver was in the habit of playing practical jokes. One evening he lay on the parlour table and got his wife to cover him with a sheet. She was then instructed to go into the bar and tell his customers he had died suddenly.

Naturally the customers expressed their condolences and the wife invited them into the parlour to pay their respects to the 'corpse'. They gathered round the table in a sympathetic silence then suddenly the 'deceased' sat up and terrified his audience. But fate was about to take a hand.

The following day the landlord was driving to Bakewell in his horse-drawn trap when the horse suddenly shied. The man was thrown and broke his neck, so that evening, he again lay on the same table, but this time he was a genuine corpse.

Various landlords have since reported hearing unexplained footsteps and being aware of an inexplicable presence. Regular visitors would not stay in one of the bedrooms and in order to find out why, a landlady and her niece slept in there one night. They occupied the double bed and a maid had a single bed in the corner. All was well until the bewitching hour of midnight when the door opened and a menacing presence entered the room. It stopped to view the occupants, walked round the bed, paused, then left the room. Could it be the ghost of that landlord playing another of his practical jokes?

The ghostly prowler

Dale Norris, landlord of the historical George Hotel at Tideswell is not unduly perturbed by the presence of their regular after-hours visitor who, according to local legend, is a lady called Sarah who skulks around the eighteenth-century pub in search of her husband.

Dale's dad Ernest was up late one night snoozing on the downstairs sofa when the sudden plummeting temperature woke him with a shiver. He glanced round and saw a woman staring over the bar. He thought she was a woman prowler until she vanished into thin air. Ernest described her as aged around fifty-five and dressed like a serving wench in a long Victorian dress and mob-cap. Others have also seen her and apparently some years ago she scared away a party of guests with her appearance and sudden disappearing trick.

The Old Bell Inn

Derby's location at almost the centre of the country made it an important coaching location. In the 1700s, there were thirty-six horse-drawn stagecoaches a day thundering through the little streets of Derby and to service these coaches, eighteen coaching inns sprang up around the centre of Derby. The best preserved example today is the Old Bell Inn in Sadler Gate, built in 1680. Haunted by many ghosts, there is a grey lady that walks around the building, a poltergeist behind the bar which throws things around and, most famous of all, the ghost in room 29, reputedly a serving wench who was murdered by Bonnie Prince Charlie's soldiers in 1745 (although there is nothing to substantiate the story).

In the 1920s room 29 was the bedroom of the landlord's son, who was an asthmatic. One night, his parents woke to hear him coughing and retching, and hurried through to his room. He was standing in the dark by his bed, bent forward and a young girl wearing an eighteenth-century costume, complete with starched apron and mob-cap, was standing over him patting his back to try to relieve his anguish. As the parents entered, the girl disappeared.

In the 1950s, room 29 was used as a nursery and the landlady at the time was changing her baby's nappy. She turned away for an instant and as she turned back to the baby, realised that she had been replaced by a serving wench who was about to pick up the baby. The mother screamed and lunged forward to grab the baby, lifting it through the apparition. Although she could still see it, she felt neither a drop in temperature or rush of air.

In 1971, Ann Jones was working as a secretary at the Bell Inn. It was 3 p.m. and the inn was closed but for two police officers who had just had lunch, the chef, the manager Nick Fay and several members of staff who had gathered in the lounge for a drink and a chat. The chef's boxer dog had also been brought in and Ann suddenly saw the dog's hair stand on end. 'His fur looked just like a hedgehog,' Ann recalled. She suddenly felt a tremendous chill and as everyone stared in disbelief,

Left: *The Old Bell Inn, Sadler Gate, Derby.* Right: *The ghost seemed to come through a closed door from this cobbled alleyway.*

a grey figure appeared. It seemed to come through a closed door from the cobbled alleyway, crossed the lounge then passed through the locked door that led to the mews and outbuildings. All those present saw the figure and Dolly Millwards the barmaid, white with shock, gave everyone a much needed whisky.

The Hardwick Inn

On 4 January 1976, eighteen-year-old Mark Gresswell and his fiancée Carol were driving through the grounds of Hardwick Hall when Carol suddenly let out a shriek of disbelief. She was sure she had just seen a ghost. She described it as wearing monk's clothing and having a brilliant white face. Mark stopped the car, and then manoeuvred it round, using the headlights to illuminate the area. While doing this another car passed and Mark then saw what he described as 'a big, tall and broad chappy' with an almost luminous face wearing monastic garb. It came towards them, then turned and disappeared into the night. Mark again tried to sweep the area with the car headlights but saw nothing.

They drove away and at the gates of the Hardwick Park pulled into the car park of the Hardwick Inn. They told their story to the landlady who confirmed that the same figure had been seen twice in the previous five days. Shortly afterwards the couple in the car that had passed them arrived and confirmed their story. They too had seen the monk.

Dot Brunt a National Trust employee who lived at nearby Stainby saw the monk on three separate occasions. He's been seen by several estate workers, two police officers and two other witnesses from Sutton in Ashfield. In fact his appearances were so numerous they were often reported in the *Derbyshire Times*.

View from the roof of Hardwick Hall looking over the grounds that are said to be haunted by a ghostly monk, Thomas Hobbes and a Cavalier.

One autumn day, a man and his dog were walking along an avenue near Hardwick Hall. The day was still, and the ankle-deep drifts of decaying leaves lay unruffled by any breath of wind. Except for the sound of their own footsteps all was silent. Suddenly the dog began to cringe with obvious fright, its coat bristled with fear and it recoiled as though from some invisible source of danger. The dog's mystified owner saw that the carpet of leaves was being stirred by invisible feet walking along the road, each step causing a fresh disturbance as the unseen pedestrian proceeded along his way.

Was this the monk taking a stroll, or could it have been the ghost of Thomas Hobbes of Malmesbury, who died at Hardwick in 1676. His portrait hangs in Hardwick Hall and his ghost is said to haunt the drive of Hardwick. There have been reports of a Cavalier too, so next time you drive through the park to admire the masterpiece created by Lady Elizabeth, Countess of Shrewsbury, more widely known as Bess of Hardwick, keep a watchful eye for those wandering ghosts too.

For the haunting stories of Bess of Hardwick, her daughter Elizabeth Cavendish and granddaughter Arbella Stuart see *Romantic Haunts of Derbyshire*.

The Sun Inn, Chesterfield

Situated just off New Square in the heart of Chesterfield, this building has been described as Chesterfield's most haunted pub. Cold spots and a peculiar atmosphere are evident in many parts; objects have moved, doors have opened and closed of their own accord and the ghost of a woman has been seen on many occasions. A family group saw her glide through the lounge; others have seen her on the stairs. One family member woke to find her standing at the bottom of her bed and on another occasion felt her bed-sheets being pulled off.

A ghostly monk is regularly seen in the grounds of Hardwick Hall.

A previous landlord was woken by sounds of strange music, and, thinking the jukebox had been left on, he hurried downstairs and immediately noticed that the unearthly sound was coming from the cellar, not the lounge. The cellar door, which he knew he had locked before going to bed, was open, but whether he went down in to the cellar to investigate is unsure. Unearthly happenings seemed to manifest themselves in the cellar of the Sun Inn, and the family's German Shepherd dog would not even go near the cellar door.

A report in the *Star* and the *Sheffield Evening Newspaper*, reported that around midnight one night in November 1957, the landlord, Mr Vincent Holmes heard a terrific crash and found empty bottles were strewn around the cellar floor. Re-stacking them, he tried to convince himself that the crates had just fallen over, but he knew this was highly unlikely.

On 16 October 1980, the *Derbyshire Times* ran the story of the hauntings of the Sun Inn, aided by the licensees at the time Stuart and Susan Hibbert. In 1986, the then landlord, Mr Les Rowlands recalled how the beer pumps had mysteriously stopped working and hurrying down to the cellar, he found the valve handles turned off. These handles were stiff to turn and no one had been down to the cellar between the beer flowing and stopping.

And things are still happening. On the morning of my visit in May 2005, the licensee Craig Sleigh had been down in the Barrel Room when he heard footsteps behind him. Thinking it was his wife Ann, he began talking to her then froze as he realised he was alone; he shot upstairs and downed a stiff drink. This was only an hour before my visit and regulars who had witnessed this were still in the bar to confirm the story told to me by Ann Sleigh. She confirmed that sounds are heard in the cellar as if a man has been locked down there, and customer's dogs (not permitted now after the considerable and attractive open-plan re-vamp) refuse to go anywhere near the cellar door. I was also told of a Victorian girl aged around ten who appears to be grounded not in the cellar, but in the upstairs of The Sun Inn. She has befriended the Sleighs' eleven-year-old daughter and the family call her a tease. She regularly moves things and has been seen sitting on the bed.

The seventeenth-century Old Sun Inn, in 1885/6. It was mostly demolished and rebuilt in 1920.

The present-day Sun Inn – note the same buildings in the background.

So why does this inn have so much paranormal activity? Some can be traced back to the time when the Sun Inn was a busy coaching inn. The basement and cellars are part of that original seventeenth-century inn, and there are in fact two capped wells in the cellar, fed by an underground spring. The story that might account for the activity in the cellar is about a coachman who had brought in a coach-load of hungry passengers. Tired and hungry, he stabled his horses and left his coach before going into the inn, but some time that evening he was murdered, probably for any money and valuables that were in his safe-keeping. His body was thrown down the well 8oft below the cellar level and no one missed him until next morning when the passengers were ready for off. No wonder the poor unfortunate coach driver is trying to alert people to his plight!

Call in the paranormal researchers

The cellars of the Devonshire Arms at Occupation Road, Newbold were investigated by the Chesterfield-based Paranormal Research Bureau after being called in by landlord Alf Matthews. 'Nobody is allowed in the cellar without my knowledge, but I've gone down there and found five beer barrels, weighing 7cwt each have been moved around. Our dog, a cross between an Alsatian and a Doberman refuses to go down there.'

Taking up the challenge to investigate, the group had an interesting time. They heard noises in the dead of night as if someone was knocking the barrels. One member felt she was being suffocated, a record flew out of the jukebox just missing two of the team and the recording equipment refused to function.

The most haunted building in Eyam

The Miner's Arms at Eyam is said to be the most haunted building in Eyam and has the plaque to prove it. That's no mean acclaim in a village where almost every cottage has a resident ghost. During the seventeenth century a woman died here after being thrown down the stairs and her ghost, dressed in an old fashioned peaked bonnet and cape, is said to wander around looking perplexed. Footsteps have been heard running along the corridors and there are strange happenings in the bedrooms, possibly the most bizarre being the manifestation of some old medical equipment which appeared one night but had gone by morning.

It's not surprising that the inn proved to be very active when investigated by a newly formed group called Strange But True. According to their secretary, Yvonne Gregory, there is much activity in the passages and a return visit is planned.

Who is that ghost?

When Phillip Richardson Wood was given a violent push which sent him sprawling over his desk, he whirled round to confront his attacker, but found that he was quite alone. Until then he might have blamed the wind for the strange noises that often sounded remarkably like footsteps walking across the floor, and the peculiarities of an old building that made the cellar door bang closed. But what caused the furniture to move, the tinkling of glasses and the feeling of being poked? These are just some of the strange happenings that people have encountered following the refurbishment of the Loft Lounge Bar in Chesterfield which has since changed hands and been renamed the Courtyard.

The building's close proximity to the graveyard of Elder Yard, Unitarian Chapel may account for some of the activity. The chapel was built in 1694 and the graveyard filled the area bordered on three

The Courtyard.

The garden at the rear of the Courtyard is a pleasant town centre oasis, but it is said also to be haunted.

Above: *Only a few gravestones dating from the end of the nineteenth century remain.*

Left: *The Elder Yard Unitarian Chapel was built in 1694 and its graveyard fills the area bordered by Knifesmithgate, Elder Way and Holywell Corss.*

sides by the buildings on Knifesmithgate, Elder Way and Holywell Cross. It was the only building that was left when the extensive Victoria Centre development took place in Knifesmithgate, but since then, on at least two separate occasions, the graveyard has been disturbed and most has now been converted into car parking.

When the Chesterfield Psychic Group investigated the hauntings at the Victoria (*see* Theatre Ghosts), Bolsover clairvoyant Edith Farrow sensed the presence of two men and two women. She felt that the two women had entered from outside and the images received were of an ornamental pond and sundial in the grounds of a large house. Her description fitted exactly with that of the ornamental garden that belonged to the old Schoolhouse, now the garden of the Courtyard Lounge Bar. This would once have been part of the Elder Yard Chapel graveyard, so could these be the same restless spirits that wander aimlessly round the area?

The favourite haunt of the pubgoers is Ashover

'Ghoulish goings on at a North Derbyshire pub are really putting customers in the Halloween spirit' reports the *Derbyshire Times* – 26 October 1995. The article related to the fifteenth-century Crispin Inn at Ashover that is rumoured to be haunted by no less than seventeen ghosts including monks, cavaliers, itinerants, animals, former landlords and children.

Early records of the Crispin, show that it was the residence of the Wall family, shoe-makers and publicans, and an apt reason for the inn's name. St Crispin is the patron saint of cobblers, saddlers and harness makers, the main occupation of most of the men of the village centuries ago.

It is one Job Wall who is immortalised in the large wall-plaque outside the inn stating that in 1646, during the Civil War, he refused admittance to the King's men, as they had had too much drink already. They ignored him, threw him out and posted a guard on the door while they drank the ale-house dry.

Jumping three and a half centuries, in July 2004 the Crispin was taken over by new owners who almost immediately set about architectural surgery. Retaining its authentic ambience, they have not only achieved a transformation that is sympathetic to the building, they have also disturbed the ghosts. Workmen have been traumatised by numerous unnerving experiences and admitted that they regularly felt something or someone behind them giving them a push.

With the completion of the work, customers have felt strange sensations, cold draughts and being touched, and on one occasion, the background music suddenly blurted out at full volume. No one had been near the music centre, yet the knob had been turned to maximum. Andrew the licensee has two young children and was convinced on one occasion that a child had thrown its arms round his legs. When he reached down and turned round, he was alone.

Ashover from the graveyard, with the Crispin Inn just outside the gates and the Black Swan in the distance.

Above: *The orb on the back wall of the dining room at the Crispin indicates a spirit presence.*

Left: *The Crispin Inn.*

Further along Church Street is the 300-year-old Black Swan where two previous licensees and family members have experienced various forms of paranormal activity. A few years ago, the landlord Simon Oxspring, saw the ghostly figure of a woman walk along an upper corridor and simply melt into the end wall. The figure was so clear, he couldn't ignore the incident and discovered that a door had previously been in that wall which divided the domestic quarters from the stables where black horses and the horse-drawn funeral hearse had previously been housed.

There have also been reports that a Cavalier haunts the upper rooms of the Black Swan but the present landlady suggests it might have simply left the Crispin because it's a bit crowded down there.

The Black Swan, where the horse-drawn funeral hearse had previously been housed.

The old pubs of Dronfield

Ashover undoubtedly has its haunted pubs, but an equally active area is the old centre of Dronfield that clusters around the church. The Blue Stoops was built in the 1590s and was originally known as the Blue Posts. It is said that the ghost of a young girl, supposedly murdered there, walks the building.

During the sixteenth century, what is now the Manor Hotel was four separate cottages, and it is in the part which was once No. 10 High Street, where visitors and staff have experienced various ghostly phenomena and sensed the friendly presence of an old lady who is believed to have lived at No. 10 at the turn of last century. She is described as being seventy years old, wearing long skirts, lace-up boots and tied back hair.

Customers have not only seen her, they have also seen the movement of brass ornaments, heard the rattle of pots and pans, been touched fleetingly and on occasions felt the old lady clinging to their arms. There is so much activity, yet the idea of calling in an exorcist is out of the question. Everyone who has experienced the hauntings feels she is a friendly spirit. The lady obviously likes the place and the company and doesn't want to leave, so next time you visit the Manor Hotel, be prepared to encounter the friendly spirit of one of their regulars.

The Green Dragon ghost has a very definite taste for certain types of beer. The thirteenth-century pub serves both real ale and keg beer, but while the cask beer remains unmolested, the others are regularly tampered with. Although all the gas cylinder taps are very stiff, they have on occasions been interfered with and even turned off.

Up to the Reformation, both the Green Dragon and the Chantry Hotel were buildings used by monks and were linked by a passage, so it's not surprising to find that they also share a paranormal spirit or two. Cylinder taps are also turned off, but more destructive, the occasional glasses are hurled through the air and plates smashed.

Four

THEATRE GHOSTS

More theatres claim to have ghosts than any other commercial enterprise. Perhaps it's the theatrical element, or perhaps it's the temperament of actors who are not aware they've had their final curtain call.

The Pomegranate Theatre

What we now know as the Pomegranate Theatre, Chesterfield, was originally the Stephenson Memorial Hall, built on part of the graveyard of the church of All Saints, better known as the Crooked Spire. Could that be one reason why not all the action at the Chesterfield Pomegranate Theatre is centred around the stage?

The Stephenson Memorial Hall, built on part of the graveyard of the Crooked Spire, seen here in the background.

Chesterfield Orchestral Society Concert in the Stephenson's Memorial Hall in the early 1900s.

Stephenson's Memorial Hall, erected by public subscription in memory of George Stephenson, cost £13,000 and opened on 14 July 1879. The building was arranged in two parts, one section comprising a public hall and the other being devoted to educational purposes. In 1889 the hall was purchased by Chesterfield Corporation, a new wing was added and for many years part of the building was used for Council purposes.

With the building of the new town hall which opened in 1939, this part of the building became Chesterfield library. The library was rehoused in the Pavements Shopping Area in the 1970s and that part of the building lay empty for nearly twenty years before, after a large scheme of redevelopment, it opened its doors as the Chesterfield Museum in May 1994.

From 1898, the other part of the building, the public hall was leased to various theatrical companies and became known as the Corporation Theatre. Plays, operas and pantomimes were presented, but by 1922, the theatre was being mainly used as a cinema with only the occasional plays and musical comedies. Four years later the theatre became exclusively a cinema, but in June 1948, the lease was not renewed. The Chesterfield Corporation resumed control and after a complete refurbishment it opened as the Civic Theatre on 19 February 1949 with a seating capacity of 622 people. In the 1980s it underwent another revamp and the name was changed to the Pomegranate Theatre.

The playful antics of the ghost of the Pomegranate Theatre have long been a talking point in theatrical circles. The friendly ghost is called George. Management, actors, caretakers, stage-hands and technicians have all witnessed strange happenings. Noises and footsteps have been heard in the upper part of the theatre when staff were certain the building was empty. On a number of occasions they have rushed upstairs to investigate the sounds and much to their vexation, have found no one there.

A caretaker was busy cleaning the floor one day when the heavy doors, the only access to the room, suddenly burst open. The force and shock of this phenomenon left him understandably

The Pomegranate Theatre.

shaken and his terror increased just minutes later when he heard footsteps descending to the lower part of the building.

Over the years, staff and management have grown accustomed to the resident ghost – thought to be the spirit of an old actor who worked at the theatre. The man was known for his love of pipe-smoking, and a distinctive feature of the hauntings is the sweet, lingering aroma of tobacco. Several eerie sightings have been reported of an elderly gentleman in a black coat and stove-pipe hat.

Theatre goers have told how seats in the auditorium mysteriously lift back to their upright position. Technicians have heard seats banging of their own accord. Most of the activities are reported to take place when the theatre is almost empty, in the early hours of the morning or after the audience has left and only the cleaning staff and caretakers are around.

The phenomena are not confined to any particular area, but seem to haunt the whole building. The dim lighting and the décor of dark bottle green accentuated with blood red, deep red velvet seats, and curtains trimmed with heavy gold braid doesn't diminish the sense of foreboding and gloom.

Next time you go to the theatre, watch out because as they say in the best pantomime tradition – 'It's behind you!'

The Hippodrome

In 1896, a theatre was built on the opposite side of the road to the Stephenson's Memorial Hall. It was originally named the Theatre Royal and was a hut-type building used as a music hall, but that was demolished in May 1896 and replaced by a permanent structure. By 1905 it began to include films as a part of the ten or so acts that comprised a programme and by 1908 acts were only used when the film reels were changed. In 1912, it became the Hippodrome. It was redecorated in 1923 and showed the first 'talkie' in 1930, but some use was still being made of the 28ft deep stage and the eight dressing rooms.

During the 1940s it was running mostly live shows and attracted many variety acts but during this time there were two deaths. One was an actor whose dressing room from then on remained locked; the other was one half of a double act who died on stage. It was always said that the friendly ghost that haunted the Hippodrome could have been either of these guys.

The theatre went into liquidation in 1950 and closed in 1954. The Hippodrome, once advertised as the prettiest theatre in Derbyshire became derelict and was later demolished to make way for the bypass.

Left: *An advertisement for the Hippodrome.*

Below: *The Hippodrome displays a 'For Sale' sign, in about the 1950s.*

The Palace

Advertised under a number of names, the Palace, the Picture Palace, and the Palace Theatre of Variety, this private venture in Burlington Street, Chesterfield opened on Monday 12 September 1910. There was no elaborate frontage on the building, just an entry next to Mr Bales ironmonger's shop on Burlington Street. But what it lacked on the outside it apparently made up for inside as the hall was comfortable with tip-up seats and for film accompaniment there was an effects machine as well as the piano. The Palace Theatre of Variety ran films with one or two variety acts to fill between the reels, but only fifteen months after its opening tragedy struck.

One of the saddest events in the history of Chesterfield occurred on 27 December 1911 at the Palace Theatre, Chesterfield. A group of young girls were waiting excitedly in a small room in an adjoining building ready to go on stage during the film intermission. They were all in costume and amongst these were Eskimo costumes made of cotton wool. Suddenly thirteen-year-old Elizabeth Bell screamed. Her costume had caught fire and flared up instantly. As her friend Ada Tidsall rushed to extinguish the flames, her own costume caught fire and pandemonium followed. Mrs Elliott the chaperone and the other girls struggled to help their panic–stricken friends but most were badly burnt in the attempt. Mr Taylor the theatre manager tried to calm the audience as the girls were rushed to hospital, but five of them died of their burns. Elizabeth (thirteen), Ada (thirteen), Lydia (twelve), Winifred (fourteen) and Mabel (thirteen). They were buried at Spital Cemetery on 1 January 1912, but they are obviously not at rest.

Inquests were held but the Palace re-opened on 6 January 1912 with mixed fare similar to before, but such a tragedy was bound to effect the reputation and popularity of the Palace. It changed hands and underwent a total renovation in 1914 to reopen as the Cinema House but as the new bigger cinemas with their full orchestras opened in the town, it seems the Cinema House simply faded away and closed in the mid-1920s.

Woolworths had become established on Burlington Street and was extended to fill the site of the demolished Cinema House. That's when customers and staff began reporting a strange atmosphere

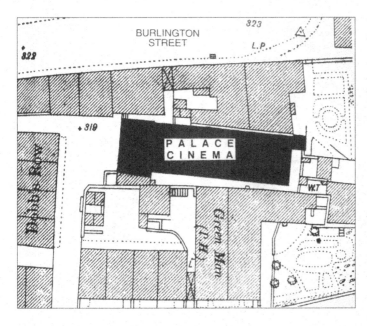

A map of chesterfield showing the old Palace Cinema.

at the back of the store, the area that coincided with the site where the disaster had occurred. Periodically there was a smell of burning and a Saturday girl weighing nails found that they were unexplainably hot.

When in 1975 a new concrete floor was laid in the basement, the workman completed the job, left his tools neatly lined up and left, locking the door behind him. Next morning when he unlocked the door the tools were in disarray and in the middle of the new floor was one single footprint. No one could find a suitable explanation. Staff refused to go in certain areas alone; people reported smelling smoke and burning, but most distressing were the screams and cries.

The Chesterfield Psychic Study Group approached the management for permission to leave detection apparatus in the store overnight but their request was met with a blank refusal. As the manager at the time said 'We do not believe in that sort of thing.'

Woolworths was demolished a few years ago to make way for new buildings, but will the echoes of the past still continue?

The Grand Theatre

The Grand Theatre on Babington Lane, Derby opened on 25 March 1886, but burnt down within a month of opening. The fire began back-stage and quickly spread to scenery and props. Actors and public were evacuated but one actor named John Adams was discovered unconscious and died on his way to hospital. The badly burnt corpse of carpenter James Locksley was later discovered by the stage door. The theatre was rebuilt and within six months had reopened, but strange happenings and stories began to circulate.

In 1924, the Grand Theatre gained notoriety for being the first theatre to stage the world premier of the stage adaptation of *Dracula* by Bram Stoker. Derby audiences were terrified by Count Dracula

The Grand Theatre is now a restaurant, but is Count Dracula on the prowl?

before any other audience in the world and as the effect was expected to be quite dramatic, St John Ambulance staff were dotted liberally amongst the audience.

Since those days, the theatre has become a nightclub and other reincarnations, but ghostly tales continue to be told. Workers refuse to go alone into certain areas, and figures have been seen in the upper storeys. Could these sightings be the ghosts of John Adams or James Locksley who so tragically lost their lives here or is Count Dracula still on the prowl?

Derby Assembly Rooms

Derby Assembly Rooms were built in 1714, enlarged in 1763 but destroyed by fire 200 years later. A much larger Assembly Rooms was opened in 1977 occupying the site on the Market Place/ Iron Gate including the site of the Duke of Newcastle's house. It now provides entertainment for Derbyshire people as well as playing host to national exhibitions and sporting events. The house manager Mick Taylor was in the building at 3 a.m. with another member of staff, standing in the concourse with his back to the Darwin Suite. For some inexplicable reason, he turned round and saw an elderly lady dressed in Victorian costume. She appeared to have no legs and seemed to be floating. Both he and his colleague witnessed her.

On many other occasions, security guards have seen what appeared to be a ring of children dancing in the Darwin Suite and have often reported the eerie sound of laughter when there is no one in the building.

The Assembly Rooms.

Victoria Cinema

The Victoria entertainment centre in Chesterfield began in the 1900s when a billiard hall was opened and part of the premises, which were behind and above adjoining shops on Knifesmithgate, were let to a cinema operator. Knifesmithgate at that time was full of small, two storey buildings, shops and inns, and the first Victoria Hall was entered down a passage just beyond the Mallet and Tool Inn. The posters for the cinema were set up on the street by the doorway of this Inn. As early as 1908 films were being run and in 1913 it was known as the Victoria Picture Palace.

During 1923 a new cinema was built at the rear of the old buildings on what had been part of the site of the Victoria foundry. Once this stage of the new build was completed, the Victoria Picture Palace was closed and torn down, together with others along the length of Knifesmithgate and the familiar Tudor-style building was erected.

This extensive new development complex which was completed in 1930 then housed not only a cinema but also the town's largest and most popular ballroom, a billiard hall, tea room and shops.
The old 'Vic' ballroom and cinema were the hub of Chesterfield's social life in their hey-day. In 1956 it was taken over by the Rank organisation, and the name of the cinema changed to Gaumont, but in January 1965 the cinema closed and was converted into a bingo hall. In more recent years, the building has been used as a supermarket.

Most of the top floor of the building – the former cinema – had become a storeroom and the whole of this floor retained a certain atmosphere. Members of staff would turn suddenly sensing someone close behind them, to find no one. Certain areas became very oppressive and regularly caused staff to suffer from headaches. Staff experienced weird sensations of unease when visiting what

The Victoria Arches a well-known town centre landmark, although there is now no sign of the Victoria Cinema.

had been the cinema's old projection room. Some felt extreme coldness and sudden clamminess. Taps turn themselves on, lights fail to work and even locked doors open and close of their own accord.

One member of staff was sent to do a stock-take in the old projection room and felt arms encircling him from behind, squeezing his body until he could hardly breathe. Total fear eventually gave him the strength to break free, but the experience had disturbed him so much he never returned to work there again. It may be that the experience was a re-enactment of a dreadful accident that occurred when the premises were occupied by the foundry. Ropes were attached to pulleys for lifting heavy goods, but somehow a rope became wrapped around the waist of one young man who was dragged up to the roof as the ever tightening rope squeezed the last breath out of him.

There are various theories as to who or what now haunts this building. Although there are no actual records to support these claims, there are many tales told of deaths at the old foundries that were previously on the site. One man was supposed to have taken his own life, and another burnt to death in the old projection room. It is also likely that the close proximity of the graveyard of the adjacent Elder Yard Chapel built in 1694 may have some connection. When a graveyard is disturbed and cleared as it was for the construction of the Victoria Centre buildings, these troubled spirits are still likely to hang around.

During 1985, the Chesterfield Psychic Study Group visited the Victoria Centre with a mixture of trepidation and anticipation. The group all experienced a strange sensation when entering the projection room and were aware of unnatural cold spots. There was a strong feeling of being watched as they moved around, almost as if they were being tracked and they were aware of similar sensations to those experienced by members of the staff.

Cineworld, Horns Bridge

Residual energy is said by some to not just exist in the fabric of a building, but to emanate from the ground upon which that building has been erected, so it is not unusual for the current residents of a site to experience the chill encounter with the paranormal that stems from some incident that happened on the site many years before.

Horns Bridge and the surrounding area where Cineworld now stands was the site of a bloody battle. The name Horns Bridge has an interesting history which could also explain why this area is so spiritually active. It goes back to the time when the Romans were advancing from the south. They had a fort at Stretton and had set up their encampment at Jawbones Hill, using stone from the Wingerworth hills to continue their road north. They were within a stone's throw of the town of Lhu-at-Adre (later Chesterfield) the southern ramparts and protective walls of which ran along the present thoroughfare known as Vicar Lane and Low Pavement. The ground which fell steeply southwards from this wall was wild and at the bottom of the slope was the River Hipper which, when confined to its banks wormed an irregular course over soft, marshy land. Undeterred the Roman road-makers began to build a bridge despite the fact that in doing so many men fell into the bog and were suffocated.

The townspeople watched the progress of the Roman soldiers, and seeing the bridge being completed made them anxious. The Britons called upon their Druid priests to help them, and through initiation by fire, Herculf the Miner was chosen to lead them against their enemy. This untrained horde of half savage Britons armed with small darts, bows and arrows, bludgeon-like staves, sharpened iron bars, keen-edged knives, sharpened spears and shields of thick animal skins made a mad rush at the well-trained, disciplined Romans who, caught by surprise, retreated under their onslaught.

At the head of the Britons was Herculf who wore a large pair of bull's horns upon his head as a sign of his rank and chieftainship, but the Romans were trained to conquer or die in the attempt, and slowly they pressed back the yelling, hysterical defenders, slaying and striking with methodical precision. Soon the River Hipper was choked with bodies and ran red with their blood.

Cineworld complex at Horns Bridge.

At the town end of the newly constructed bridge which was wide enough to allow four men abreast to pass, Herculf, surrounded by his men, made one heroic last stand. The Roman soldiers crowded the bridge and many of them fell over the sides into the surging water below.

'The Bull's Horns shall win the victory for us or I die,' cried Herculf. 'If I fall take thee my place Barnold and wear these horns of mine, for this bridge and this place of battle shall hereafter be known to all our countrymen as the battle of the Horns Bridge and these marshes shall hereafter be called the Horns Fields.'

Herculf fought heroically until falling exhausted, he was swept into the river and drowned. The Britons, now leaderless fled towards the town, the Romans regained the bridge and proceeded victoriously north, but from then on, as Herculf had wished, the bridge took the name he had designated – Horns Bridge.

For many years, stories circulated about strange happenings and appearances around Horns Fields. People regularly spoke about the mysterious figure of a man who disappeared through the wall at Horns Bridge. Apparently on one occasion, a man was walking his dog in the area when the dog shot off towards the bridge as though chasing someone or something, running headlong into the solid brick wall, causing severe facial injuries. The old Horns Bridge signal box was also reputedly haunted as was the site formerly occupied by the Tube Works and the Alma Public House.

The site is now a modern leisure centre complete with multiplex cinema where staff have reported strange inexplicable sightings. The projection room from where the apparatus beams the images onto the screen seems to be the most spiritually active. Staff have seen movements and sensed the feeling of being watched. One staff member distinctly heard her name being called and few venture into the dimly lit projection room alone.

*A 1980s advertisement for the
Derby Playhouse, Eagle Centre.*

The Derby Playhouse

Derby Playhouse opened in the Eagle Centre in 1975. Workers have since experienced the ghost of a woman in the ladies toilets and members of the public have experienced blasts of cold air and a feeling of being watched. A man in black seen around the bar and restaurant has been mistaken for a member of bar staff until he simply disappears. One of the dressing rooms is said to be haunted, but staff are keeping mum on this one to avoid upsetting any contemporary actors.

The Derby Hippodrome

The Derby Hippodrome is just a few yards from the Grand Theatre, on the corner of Green Lane and Macklin Street. It opened in 1914 as a 2,300 capacity music-hall-style venue attracting such great names as Gracie Fields, George Formby, Max Miller and Flanagan and Allen. It is said that Bud Flanagan composed 'Underneath the Arches' during one of his visits to Derby while sheltering under the railway bridge in Ford Street. But it is not great names of stage and variety that haunt this particular theatre. This theatre was built on the site of Derby's first private lunatic asylum, which closed shortly after a shocking incident where one of the inmates cut a warder's throat. The staggering apparition of this warder, clutching his throat and covered in blood has been seen in this building.

The Derby Hippodrome.

The impressive Guildhall.

The Guildhall

The Guildhall Theatre may owe its paranormal activity to the fact that in its foundations are a labyrinth of tunnels and catacombs, one of which used to link the old police lock-up in Lock-Up Yard to the Assize Court in the Guildhall. Many people have reported hearing the sound of trudging feet along these tunnels, a play-back to those earlier days when prisoners would have passed through here on their way to be executed. But even more strange, council staff wandering the labyrinth of tunnels often see a child who they have named little Sammy.

And just be warned ladies! A woman visiting the loo heard a tune being hummed in a neighbouring cubicle despite the fact that she thought she was alone. Leaving the cubicle, she realised she was, the neighbouring cubicle was empty and no one had left the room.

Buxton Opera House

The Pavilion Gardens in the centre of Buxton was opened in 1871 with the addition of a complex of buildings in the form of a miniature Crystal Palace in 1876, with the Opera House added some thirty years later. It is a wonderful building designed by theatre architect Frank Matcham and features elaborate interior decoration, but does it also house a ghost?

Some people say it does, while the various strange happenings at the Buxton Opera House leave others unsure. Apart from the usual noises that can set active imaginations racing, theatre staff have witnessed lights going on and off without warning and a kettle boiling of its own accord. It is featured in the town's ghost walks, but some guides who conduct these walks keep them deliberately light-hearted so as not to upset anyone. Buxton's guided walk is conducted with more humour than horror and revealed nothing that might answer the question – Is Buxton Opera House actually haunted?

Five

GRAVEYARD GHOSTS

Churchyards, where the stage is set for the last act of human drama, are the natural theatre for ghosts. Some even have what have become known as cemetery lights that hover over graves after dark as bluish balls of light.

Also known as corpse candles or spook lights, in the olden days these flickering lights were believed to be caused by the soul, which detaches itself from the physical body at death, and can occasionally be seen as a glowing light. The size of the light indicates the age of the person; the larger the light, the older the person. If the colour of the flame is white, it's a woman, if red, a man.

Safeguarding the graveyard from the Devil

According to tradition, the first person to be buried in a graveyard returned in spirit to protect the dead from the Devil, demons and other nefarious supernatural creatures that may haunt such places.

One such creature was the ghoul, a nasty, vicious-looking ghost believed to gain sustenance from eating the flesh of corpses. Hence a ghoul is often described as a ghost that haunts graveyards. Then there was the two legged wingless lindorm, a sort of dragon/serpent. Supposedly lindorms were commonly encountered in churchyards where they devoured human corpses. It is easy therefore to see why the task of guarding a graveyard was so great. That's why, before any human was interred, tradition stated that a black dog should be buried alive in the grounds of a newly built church, thus creating a guardian spirit, known as the kirke-grim or church grim. 'Grim' is a generic name for a spirit which associates with humanity and human dwellings, and the church grim will never leave its designated graveyard. A church grim has been seen around St Peter's church at Chellaston. It's described as being a huge, bear-like creature with a dirty, mangy coat. It seems to appear from thin air and walks silently in and around the graveyard, often pausing to survey its witnesses with large saucer–like glowing eyes before disappearing again.

It is thought that the church grim originated from the pagan practice of sacrificing an animal at a place of worship. Making a foundation sacrifice when a church was built or a churchyard consecrated was one of a number of pagan practices which lasted into the early Christian era. Although we know that the job of the church grim was to protect and guard the church and graveyard, unfortunately we are not enlightened as to how. Did it attack psychologically or physically? Perhaps its presence alone was enough to make the area frightening and intimidating to demonic forces and humans alike.

I went on a ghost walk in Eyam, Derbyshire's notorious plague village, and we arrived at the graveyard at 10 p.m. People consider graveyards to be conducive to hypnotic suggestion and fright, and the spookiest places after dark, but as there was quite a group of us, I thought there was safety in numbers. I stood at the front of the church by the side of the impressive tomb of Catherine Mompesson, the wife of the Revd William Mompesson, who at the outbreak of the plague in

Castleton graveyard, where a white misty shape floats in the branches of the tree on the left. Can you see the features of a face?

September 1665 persuaded all the villagers to remain within the village to stop the plague spreading. Catherine's ghost is said to haunt the rectory and walk between there and the graveyard.

I felt nothing until we walked round to the huge graveyard at the back of the church. That's when I started to experience the most bizarre and unaccountable sensations. I felt an increasing build up of pressure across my forehead and behind my ears as if I was wearing too tight a hat that was getting tighter and tighter by the second. I tried to be rational but my ears were drumming and my head was swimming. I knew that if I stayed there, I would pass out, but as soon as I decided to leave, the sensation vanished. I was in the area where in broad daylight, people have regularly reported seeing a little girl dancing round the gravestones.

It was mid afternoon when I went for a walk round Castleton graveyard and experienced one of my scariest moments. I was looking for a good angle to take a photograph of Peveril Castle perched on the hill, with a few gravestones in the foreground for effect. There was no one around and I'd just taken a few shots when just behind me I heard a clink, clank like clashing chains. I whirled round but saw nothing, although I'm not too sure what I expected to see; perhaps some fettered phantom Jacob Marley style.

Rasping with relief, I'd almost decided to file this under incidents with no logical explanation when it sounded again and my eyes shot to the flagpole. I walked over, eyes fixed. I plucked the rope and as it twanged back and hit the metallic flagpole the sound was repeated exactly. I'd physically had to pluck the rope, so what had happened earlier? There was no one else in the vicinity, no wind, and no explanation until I looked at one of my photographs later, and there, floating over a gravestone was a white misty shape. As I looked closer, I realised I could see a definite face. It had dark features, a heavy jaw, receding hairline and prominent ears. Was this a phantom who had summoned up all it's power to make contact?

The footless ghost of Bakewell churchyard

The path that leads through Bakewell churchyard is regularly used by locals as a shortcut to and from the town. One evening a couple of lads had been in Bakewell and were walking home through the churchyard, which is on quite a steep hill, when they paused by a gravestone to catch their breath and have a cigarette. They were just about to proceed when they saw a man dressed in black coming through the lych gate on Church Lane. He began to glide towards them and they stared in horror because, although he wore a tall hat which seemed to give him extra height, his feet were missing. This would indicate that he was actually walking on the old path that would have been lower in his time prior to it being tarmaced.

North Wingfield

Draped in traditional brown robes, the Mad Monk that haunts North Wingfield Churchyard is said to be crazed.

North Wingfield graveyard.

He has been seen wandering around, drifting between the rows of graves clutching a large wooden cross. The Mad Monk reputedly appears at exactly 2.30 a.m. looming out from the front of the church, but it seems he resents the intrusion of mere mortals. Early one morning, three members of the Paranormal Research Bureau were positioned at strategic observation points near the church when they all felt a sudden inexplicable compulsion to get away from the cemetery.

They felt as if a disturbing presence seemed to cling to them, then, without warning, one of the guys began to recite Latin. This was totally alien. He had never read or spoken Latin. His eyes became distant and still, his face pale and drawn, his body trembled with cold and fear, and his voice was almost unrecognisable.

He was clearly overcome by a strong physical force and it was ten minutes or more before he returned to normal. He later told his colleagues that he had felt a tremendous pressure around him, which he was unable to fight.

St Edmund's spiritual tree

The graveyard of St Edmund's, Allestree is another haunted by a monk in black habit who walks hastily towards the church and vanishes through the stonework. More unusually, it also appears to have a spiritual yew tree which is believed to be around 1,000 years old. In late Autumn when other trees have shed their leaves, this ancient Yew is said to be heard whispering and groaning, and if you place your ear to the trunk they say you can hear a heartbeat.

The artistic St Wilfred's

The churchyard of St Wilfred's at Barrow on Trent is haunted by the ghost of George Turner the nineteenth-century famous watercolorist who once lived at an old farmhouse called the Walnuts. But George is no midnight spirit. Rather artistically, he has reportedly been seen on warm summer evenings with brush and easel seated as if painting the church.

Ashover graveyard ghost

Not so many years ago, nothing would induce the inhabitants of Ashover to go through the churchyard after dark, because of the ghost. It was said to be in the form of a headless woman. Who she is and why she is headless is unknown, but in times past, it was common practise to decapitate the dead in order to stop their spirits rising from the grave. Archaeological excavations of many Pagan, Celtic and Saxon burials have revealed that the heads of some of the remains had been removed and placed between their knees or feet.

Alternatively, she could be the ghost of the wife of John Towndrow, a sixty-year-old farmer from Milltown who on 10 June 1841 bludgeoned her to death, cut off her head, then slit his own throat.

What makes this story rather different is the strange twist that occurred when in the mid-nineteenth century during a dinner party at Stubben Edge Hall a wager was made that no one dare go to the churchyard and bring back a skull. Macabre though this now sounds, it was once the fashion to collect and display unusual and grotesque artefacts, the more macabre the piece of ornamentation the better, and skulls were much in demand. The story of Dicky Tunstead, a skull that acted as a cranial guardian of a farm overlooking Coombes reservoir up in the High Peak for 350 years, gained national acclaim for its supposed antics.

At the time there was also a widely practiced belief in the science of phrenology, the study of the shape and size of the skull to determine the strength of various mental faculties. Whatever the reason for making the wager, it was taken up by one of the party, said to be one of the Milnes family who lived at the Hall, who went to the graveyard and secured a skull.

During the building of a conservatory at Stubben Edge Hall in 1889, this skull was found and caused much conjecture as to the reason for its presence. It was returned to the churchyard and it would seem that the ghost of Mrs Towndrow could at last rest in peace as the last official sighting of the headless ghost was in 1890 when she is said to have been standing in the north aisle of the church at about 8 o'clock in the evening.

An empty stone coffin, dating from around 1200 was unearthed in Ashover churchyard many years ago, and supposedly if you walk round it three times, then lie in it with your eyes closed, you will hear the ghostly sounds of rattling chains. I went to check this out for myself on a bright sunny day, but my plans were thwarted. I found the empty stone sarcophagus lying at the base of the church tower, but as it is too close to the church wall, there was no way anyone could walk round it.

A stone coffin in Ashover graveyard.

Ashover graveyard.

Duffield Church built by the Devil

According to local legend, St Alkmund's Church at Duffield has the rare distinction of being sited by the Devil. Apparently, the site of the church was initially chosen to be near the ruined Duffield Castle as the material from this was to be used to build the church. Building commenced and the foundation stones were laid but when the builders returned the following day, they found the materials had been moved to a different location at the other end of the village. The mystified builders returned the materials to the chosen site and work continued but the same thing happened again.

Despite all their efforts the building was not progressing and rumours began to circulate that it was the Devil at work. The people said that evil spirits occupied the site and the Devil would never allow it to be used for religious purposes. Undeterred, prayers were said over the site and the materials, but to no avail. The materials continued to be moved so eventually the builders gave up and built the church on the other site where the church still stands.

St Peter's Church

St Peter's Church in the centre of Derby dates back to 1046 and served the most densely populated part of the town, so it's not surprising that in its churchyard are more dead bodies than in any other graveyard in Derby. Many were buried standing up, to ease the overcrowding.

In 1349, the Black Death killed one third of the population of Derby. People thought the plague was passed from one person to another, so as soon as a person was dead, you were buried in haste. Unfortunately, one of the symptoms of the plague was a long deep sleep or coma and many folks were buried prematurely. There are reports in St Peter's parish register of hands appearing out of the soil and clawing their way out of their shallow graves.

The Count Dracula story originated from such stories, and in 1924, the world premier of the play 'Count Dracula' was performed in Derby at the Grand Theatre on Babington Lane.

St Alkmund's Church at Duffield.

St Peter's churchyard, where hands are said to claw their way out of shallow graves.

Derby Cathedral

Although All Saint's church didn't become Derby Cathedral until 1927 it was actually built around 943. When the 212ft tower was added in 1527 it was the second tallest parish church in England, yet the church fell into disrepair, and apart from the tower, was rebuilt under the design of James Gibbs, more famous for his building of St Martin-in-the-Fields in Trafalgar Square, London.

This 'ordinary' church became a cathedral at a time when there was neither time nor money to build the style of grand cathedral like there are in many major cities. Despite having very little in

Derby Cathedral: the haunt of many unhappy ghosts.

the way of a graveyard, it is still reportedly haunted by a few ghosts. The most notable is said to be Charles Edward Stuart, although why is unsure. This unfortunate gentleman only visited briefly on one occasion in 1745. Another ghost is the ubiquitous white lady seen walking down the steps at the back, and a small boy.

Also said to wander the grounds is the unhappy ghost of John Crossland, a criminal turned traitor. He was offered his freedom if he agreed to hang his father and brother. He did and from then on became the busiest executioner in the area. It is unlikely that this less than Christian soul should be buried here, so his dubious presence holds another big question mark.

Mapperley

There is an unmarked grave in Mapperley churchyard that hides a sad story of lost love. This is the last resting place of Giles Kidbrooke, a Mapperley soldier who fought in the Crimean War. Before leaving, Giles proposed to his sweetheart Kate Usher and they made plans to be married when he returned, so imagine Kate's reaction when she heard that her soldier-fiancé had been killed in action. The heartbroken girl could not be comforted and shortly afterwards, her drowned body was found in Mapperley pond. The verdict of the inquest was that she had committed suicide.

Ironically, the information that her fiancé was dead was incorrect. Giles had been badly wounded and it was some time before he recovered sufficiently to return home to Mapperley. Hearing the news of Kate's death, he was devastated, died within the year and was buried in the churchyard, but he is not at peace. His ghost is said to appear every year on 25 October, the anniversary of Kate's death, vainly seeking his lost love.

The grieving girl at Hazelwood

To celebrate the Queen's Silver Jubilee in 1977, the village of Hazelwood held a celebratory party in the village hall. Peter Booth, his wife Carol and daughter Anne drove down from their farm cottage and parked by the wall at the side of the churchyard. Another car pulled in behind them. The Booth family noticed the man who had got out of the second car staring at something in the graveyard, a strange expression on his face. They asked if he was alright.

'I think I may just have seen a ghost!' he said, then proceeded to tell them how he had glanced over the wall and seen a young woman dressed in white, kneeling by a grave. Her arm was on a tombstone and her forehead rested on her arm. She was lost in grief. She was so clear he had noticed the buttons down the back of her dress and her strikingly long auburn hair.

As usually happens, news of this spread and other people confessed to seeing the ghost of the grieving girl. Two ladies attending a funeral had fainted when they saw her.

Peter told his sister Gwen Watts who, many years later, was driving past the graveyard with Ruth, her son's girlfriend. Gwen related the story of the grieving girl expecting Ruth, who was a rational young woman to make some witty comment, but she didn't. The girl's silence made Gwen turn to look at her and Ruth's face was white. She then confessed that while driving alone past the graveyard in June 1988 she had glanced over and seen the grieving girl. She too described the long auburn hair and the long white dress with buttons down the back, but on this occasion the spectre was clutching a posy of flowers to her chest, and weeping. Ruth had been so touched by the girl's grief she had looked away, but when she looked back, the figure had disappeared.

The crying angel at Etwell

Unlike the young woman who is seen at Hazelwood graveyard in broad daylight, the ghostly figure of a woman who haunts Etwell graveyard makes her appearances at night. People who have walked past the graveyard late at night have heard sobbing, but many believe this is not a ghost but the marble statue of a crying angel that stands in a corner of the graveyard. What's more, they say that at night she comes alive and wanders round the graveyard looking at headstones.

Thomas Beckett at Ticknall

The picturesque ruins of the old church of Thomas Beckett at Ticknall still stand and at the gothic window with its stone tracery has been seen the kneeling figure of a lady in blue, deep in prayer. There is also a wailing, golden-haired child dressed in the clothes of the Elizabethan era, who when approached vanishes.

Wingerworth

Gwen and David White and their border collie Sammy were walking through Wingerworth graveyard one evening when suddenly a figure swelled up in front of them before disappearing into a yew tree. Sammy who had been charging around, stopped stock still with his ears pricked up, staring at the spot.

'Did you see that?' asked David in disbelief.

'I did,' replied Gwen and was able to describe the phantom as a man wearing black trousers and a white shirt with sleeves rolled up to his elbows although unnervingly, he was semi-transparent.

Wingerworth graveyard.

Eyre Chapel.

Eyre Chapel

The Eyre Chapel at Newbold, Chesterfield is tiny; it measures only 36ft by 16ft. It was built as a chapel of ease in the thirteenth century, and became associated with the Eyre family who were predominantly Roman Catholics. Throughout the centuries, Roman Catholics have been persecuted for their faith and on frequent occasions, this little chapel was systematically ransacked, frequently destroyed and the tombstones removed to use in local buildings. Now the chapel has been restored, and around it is the grassy remains of its churchyard where strange sights and sounds have been reported.

The chapel is situated behind the Nags Head public house on Newbold Road and people living there have experienced what they describe as echoing sounds like chanting, which is often accompanied by strange lights and the indistinct shape of a hooded figure.

Chesterfield Crooked Spire

The graveyard of Chesterfield's Crooked Spire has been reduced drastically since its construction, which began in the early thirteenth century. Now the heavy traffic on the A61 rattles past its eastern side, but a small section of the graveyard still exists on the north, south and west sides.

Well-used paths cut through the graveyard linking the museum, the Pomegranate and the railway station with the main part of town. It was along one of these paths that two young women were walking one evening. There was a slight mist swirling, but both saw a brown-robed figure by the church wall apparently peering in through one of the windows.

Crooked Spire – No one could see through the windows because of the drainage ditch.

A week later, taking the same path through the churchyard, they again glanced in the direction where they had seen the figure. It was only then that they realised that a deep, 5ft drainage ditch separated the churchyard from the wall. It would have been totally impossible for anyone to stand and look through the church window, or at least it would have been impossible for any human!

Holy Trinity churchyard

The churchyard of the Holy Trinity church, Chesterfield, stretches between Newbold Road and Sheffield Road so it is not surprising that for many years this has been used as a shortcut between the two. In broad daylight, a pupil at St Helen's school hurrying through the churchyard saw a white misty shape. It apparently had no firm outline but was about the size of an adult and appeared to be leaning against the entrance gates on Sheffield Road; as she watched, the shape slowly disappeared yet she felt no fear only bewilderment.

During the Second World War, a young man had a similar experience. He lived in Whittington Moor and was employed by the L.M.S. Railway as a fireman at the Hasland Shed. He travelled to and from work during the night and it was particularly dark because of the blackout. Passing the Sheffield Road gates on his way to an early morning shift, he noticed the white clad figure of an old lady. He dismounted and asked if she was alright but she neither answered nor turned round, but just disappeared into the trees. It had been 2.30 a.m. and when he told his work mates they laughed at him. However, the following morning he saw her again standing between the two stone gateposts, and this time he noticed that she held a crucifix in her hand. He again stopped to ask if she was alright and if she had walked through the churchyard the previous morning. She said she had and as he saw no reason to prolong the conversation, the man rode away.

When relating this story for the Chesterfield Psychic Study Group many years later, he was still unsure whether she had been a harmless, eccentric old lady or a ghost.

The gates of Holy Trinity – said to be haunted by a figure in white.

The rising corpses

This is undoubtedly the strangest story ever and, if it hadn't been written by such an eminent man, would have undoubtedly been considered pure unadulterated fiction. However, the facts were written in a letter by a Dr James Clegg, a worthy, down-to-earth, Non-Conformist minister of Chapel en le Frith, to his close colleague, the Revd Dr Ebenezer Latham. Dr Clegg was a man of some learning and was the author of *The Life of the Rev John Ashe*, a biography of the religious writer and dissenting minister of Ashford who died in 1735. This kind of serious commitment to writing gives credence to the letter, yet still doesn't make it any less puzzling:

> I know you are pleased with anything curious or uncommon in nature, and if what follows shall appear such, I can assure you from eye witnesses of the truth of every particular.
>
> In a Church at about three miles distance from us, the indecent custom still prevails of burying the dead in a place set apart for the Devotion of the Living; yet the parish not being very populous, one would scarce imagine the inhabitants of the grave could be strai'tned for want of room; yet it would seem so, for on the last day of August, several Hundreds of Bodies rose out of the grave in the open day in that Church, to the great astonishment and Terror of several spectators.
>
> They deserted the Coffin, and arising out of the grave, immediately ascended directly towards Heaven, singing in Concert all along as they mounted thro' the Air; they had no winding sheets about them, yet did not appear quite naked, their Vesture seem'd streak'd with gold, interlaced with sable, skirted with white, yet thought to be exceeding light by the agility of their motions, and the swiftness of their ascent. They left a most fragrant and delicious odour behind them, but were quickly out of sight, and what is become of them or in what distant regions of this vast system they have since fixed residence, no Mortal can tell…
>
> The Church is in Heafield, three miles from Chappel Frith. 1745.

The shocking affair at Chapel en le Frith

The black hole of Calcutta has made its mark in history, yet we have an incidence which is no less barbaric and terrible on our own doorstep, and what makes this even more detestable is that this 'black hole' was a church.

On 14 September 1648, 1,500 Scottish soldiers taken prisoners at the battle of Ribble Moor near Preston were herded into the tiny church at Chapel en le Frith and the doors securely locked. The men were imprisoned for sixteen days without food, water or even sufficient space to lie down. It was 30 September before they were released from the confines of their tiny prison. Forty-four of the soldiers were dead and many were dying. They were buried in the churchyard, so is there any surprise that the haunted feeling in the graveyard of Chapel en le Frith is one of utter despair and misery. It sounds intangible, but people who have experienced it say that it is unmistakable.

St Oswald

Positioned on the gateposts of Ashbourne's historical church of St Oswald are huge pyramids resting on stone skulls. Some people may view these as decorative, but is there something more sinister in their use? Heads were revered by our Celtic ancestors because a person's spirit was believed to be held in the head. By lopping off their enemies heads, it was believed they had not only defeated him, they would also possess his spirit. On Hallowe'en or Shaim Armein, the spirits become free, so to entice them back, a lighted taper or candle was put inside the skull. This is the derivation of the Hallowe'en pumpkin, hollowed out and cut to represent a skull with a candle burning inside.

Skulls on the gateposts at Ashbourne church.

The churchyard of St Oswald is said to be the haunt of three haggard-looking ghosts, dressed in sackcloth and thought to have been victims of the plague. A ghost child is often seen wandering around the gravestones and standing close to the main gate. She is believed to be Penelope Boothby who died in 1791 aged six. Her magnificent tomb inside Ashbourne church depicts this beautiful child in slumber.

St Wystan

St Wystan church at Repton is the haunt of many ghosts. The fourteenth-century tower and recessed church spire harbours the mischievous spirit of a goblin who appears when there is a full moon. If caught, he will grant mortals one wish, provided it is made there and then, and the wish does not benefit the person.

The Saxon crypt of St Wystan is believed to have held the body of St Wystan. It is also the haunt of a hooded, monk-type figure, a humming ghost and a more demonic figure bathed in wreaths of smoke, who has also been seen sitting on a gravestone in the churchyard.

The ghostly figure of a man has been seen placing flowers on a grave just to the right of the south porch. It is said to be James Wheldon, the repentant killer of twenty-one-year-old Samuel Marshall who was murdered in 1786. Wheldon was caught but acquitted at trial through the lack of witnesses.

A seventeenth-century gravedigger is also reported to haunt the area around the church. At one time, he would stand in the trees at the edge of the graveyard and watch the village gravedigger as he worked. Pupils from the school that overlooks part of the churchyard have seen ghosts wander between the graves then mysteriously disappear. Could they vanish into the tunnel that according to legend runs from the graveyard to Anchor Church, an impressive cave structure said to be haunted by at least one monk?

St Wystan's, Repton.

Repton School looks over the graveyard.

Hathersage

The church in the historical village of Hathersage (written Hereseige in 1086) is dedicated to the dragon-slaying St Michael. The hillside site where the church now stands was probably sacred before the arrival of the first Christian missionaries in the Hope Valley, but this has to be the most visited graveyard in Derbyshire because it is the last resting place of Little John, the right-hand man of the legendary outlaw Robin Hood.

After Robin's death at Kirklees, Little John probably wandered around aimlessly, lost in more ways than one, and upon reaching Hathersage collapsed from exhaustion. His grave which lies in the churchyard just opposite the main door has huge yew trees at each end and is marked by three stone slabs. The current headstone informs the reader that 'Here Lies Buried Little John, The Friend & Lieutenant of Robin Hood. He died in a cottage (now destroyed) to the east of the churchyard.'

Little John's grave was opened in 1728 and bones of an enormous size were found in it. In the late eighteenth century it was opened again and a thigh bone 32in long was exhumed and put on display by Captain Shuttleworth, brother of the local squire. Unlike the story of skulls that act as talismans to bring good fortune and avert danger, this thigh bone seemed to be doing just the opposite, so the Captain decided that the bone was a source of bad luck and gave it to the parish clerk to arrange for it to be re-buried. Hopefully this was carried out and Little John was once again allowed to rest in peace.

St Mary's churchyard

Sutton Scarsdale Hall presents a sad, melancholy appearance despite the fact that it was once an outstanding example of Classical architecture. Now owned by English Heritage, the site retains an air of ghostly quiet so it's not surprising to find that there are numerous stories of ghosts that haunt the hall and the annexed Church of St. Mary on the site.

A man walking his dog along a narrow path through the graveyard at midday noticed how the dog's ears were erect and the hair on his back was standing on end. Its head moved as if following the movement of something passing between an old entrance from the Hall and the church, then it charged off, sniffing the ground as it ran to the church entrance.

The Chesterfield Psychic Research Society have visited Sutton Scarsdale Hall and church during daylight and at night, and on one occasion they saw a grey-looking figure appear and walk towards the back of the church. As they hurriedly followed, their footsteps disturbed the rustling leaves, yet the grey figure made no sound as it walked, then disappeared round the corner of the building.
When investigated by a newly formed group called Strange But True, secretary Yvonne Gregory reported that a spirit threw stones at them.

One story that had amazing repercussions originated as a bet between a Nottingham professor and a resident of Hillstown. The professor agreed to pay the man £1 if he agreed to be fastened to a post in the graveyard and to remain there past the bewitching hour of midnight. The man took up the bet, but alone in the dark in such eerie surroundings, his courage failed him; he broke free and ran. The terrified man claimed that he had seen a ghost with no legs and wearing a white hood with slits for the eyes, glide through the graveyard.

Understandably this story flew round the neighbourhood, probably gaining much in the telling until local ghost hunters flocked to the churchyard to see the 'white lady'. An article appeared in the *Star* newspaper on 29 June 1967 and quoted the Rector of St Mary's, who suggested that the ghost could possibly be one of the white owls that glide between the graveyard's bushes and trees. Despite this possible explanation, there is much to suggest that Sutton Scarsdale churchyard is very haunted.

The Hathersage grave of Little John.

HERE LIES BURIED

LITTLE JOHN
THE FRIEND & LIEUTENANT OF
ROBIN HOOD
HE DIED IN A COTTAGE (NOW DESTROYED)
TO THE EAST OF THE CHURCHYARD
THE GRAVE IS MARKED BY
THIS OLD HEADSTONE & FOOTSTONE
AND IS UNDERNEATH THIS OLD YEW TREE

Sutton Scarsdale.

Alternative gravesite haunts

The earthly remains of most of our forebears used to be laid to rest in the local graveyard, yet there are exceptions. During the seventeenth century there was a shroud tax levied on burials in public churchyards, so to avoid this, house-burials were known in many parts of the Peak District. It's also possible that some house-burials followed earlier beliefs that no building would be secure until a living creature was interred in the foundations.

There are also alternative gravesites. Lying in isolation one mile outside Ashford in the Water on the road to Monsall Head is a nineteenth-century burial plot, like a roadside oasis surrounded by flat fields. Edged with mature trees and a stone wall, this is the Infidels Cemetery, so named because the gravestones apparently have no reference to God. I was unable to verify this as the rampant vegetation has almost swallowed them up and the plot is well protected by a stone wall and substantial fencing. This was once thought to be the burial place of evil people, and the fact that it is said to be haunted by a vampire, a grey lady and a man in black has compounded its reputation.

Plague sites

In order to stop the spread of infection, plague victims were often buried hurriedly without any form of religious ceremony in fields and waste ground near to their homes. The Hancock family graves at Riley Farm, Eyam is one such example. Here, Mrs Hancock buried seven members of her own family in the middle of a field next to her home. The site, high on the hillside above Eyam, is now ringed by a protective stone wall. It is possible to visit these graves, but don't be surprised if you encounter Mrs Hancock. She was the only surviving member of the family and is probably still visiting their graves, because a woman in a blue dress is said to haunt the Riley Graves.

When the plague decimated whole communities, individual burial was often impossible, so any number of bodies would be heaped into a communal grave with no record of who they were or when they died. These burial grounds were subsequently declared hallowed ground and disturbing them is still frowned up. It is because of one of these plague pits which now appears as a mound in the land close to Brimington, that the Chesterfield Canal had to deviate from its straight course in order to avoid cutting straight through it. Although few people know about the plague pit, many describe this scenic section of towpath beside the canal as eerie, even in the daylight.

Watery Grave

But what makes this area doubly eerie is that in the same vicinity as the plague pit, on 24 March 1886, a murder took place. Thirty-nine-year-old Herbert Crooks was married with five children, and lived at Rosene House Farm, Cutthorpe. He was a prosperous farmer, owned a butcher's shop at Clowne and was in the process of buying another at Killermarsh. He had just visited the Killermarsh premises and was on his way home following the path of the Chesterfield Canal when he was violently attacked and robbed in Bluebank Wood, Brimington. His body was then callously dumped in the murky waters of the Chesterfield Canal. Three men on their way to work at 5.40 the next morning found his body floating in the backwater of the Wheeldon Mill Lock, but his killers were never found and his death remains unavenged.

In the 1970s two boys from Brimington were walking along a lane behind King Street when a tall man wearing a flat crowned top hat and a long dark coat seemed to materialise out of the shadows. There was something out of the ordinary about him, and the boys were deeply distressed and ran home.

Arthur Skelhorn, a Brimington resident regularly took his dog for an early evening walk along the banks of the canal, but one cold winter evening in 1993 it was much later than his usual time. A mist had risen off the water and the air was cold as he headed down Newbridge Lane and towards the Canal Bank. Mr Skelhorn noticed the man standing approximately 20yds in front of him. He was over 6ft tall and wearing a large top hat and a dark coat which seemed to trail the ground. Mr Skelhorn was wary but reasoned that the man might be lost and wanting directions so saw no reason to avoid walking towards him. What he was surprised to notice was that his dog who normally runs ahead, stayed close by his side. As Mr Skelhorn walked round the mound of land that marks the plague pit, he realised that the man had gone and the 150yds straight towpath was completely empty, but it was simply not possible for a man to disappear in such a short space of time. The experience so shook him that Mr Skelhorn vowed never again to go back to that area of the canal after dark.

So could the mystery man who walks the banks of the Chesterfield Canal be Herbert Crooks looking to take his own form of revenge, or one of the poor unfortunate, un-named victims of the plague who were so hastily and unceremoniously buried there?

Crossroads

Murderers, suspect witches and suicides who could not be interred in consecrated ground, were traditionally buried at crossroads to emphasise their marginal status in society. There is also the Christian belief that crossroads were used because the cross was a form of protection from vampires, demons and supernatural night creatures. Just to be on the safe side, the poor unfortunates whose last resting place was a crossroads were often buried with a stake thrust through them in an attempt to keep their spirits from wandering. It didn't seem to do much good as crossroads seem to be a favourite haunt of ghosts. Riders are always cautious at crossroads because horses can sense spirits and tend to shy there, so if you are on horseback, on foot or in your car, do watch out!

Other titles published by The History Press

Romantic Haunts of Derbyshire

JILL ARMITAGE

This fascinating collection of tales reveals the region's darkest and most tragic love affairs. Delve into sad stories of thwarted lovers, unrequited passions and broken hearts, with betrayals, suicides, and murderous rivals, and discover the host of paranormal activity that may be the result of these doomed romances. From sightings of shadowy figures and spirits, to moving objects, unexplained sounds and bloodstains that cannot be removed, this selection covers all aspects of paranormal – and romantic – activity in the county.

978 0 7524 4651 6

Ghost Pets & Spirit Animals

JILL ARMITAGE

Ghost enthusiasts and pet lovers can combine their passion in this unique publication which will make a most absorbing read for animal lovers and those interested in the paranormal. With chapters including 'Can your Pet see Ghosts?', 'Spectral Horses', 'Black Dogs' and 'Ghostly Hounds', this book contains around 160 individual spooky anecdotes illustrated by a number of atmospheric photographs and also some, apparently, depicting ghost animals!

978 0 7524 3997 6

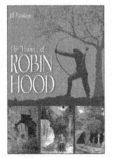

The 'Haunts' of Robin Hood

JILL ARMITAGE

This fascinating volume searches for the ghosts of Merrie Men long gone amongst the trees of Sherwood and beyond, through Nottinghamshire, Derbyshire, Yorkshire and into Staffordshire. From hidden caves to ancient abbeys, it discovers the places mentioned in the early ballads and the ancient sites and buildings traditionally associated with this famous legendary figure, as well as something less tangible, but just as real: the ghosts who haunt them.

978 0 7524 4331 7

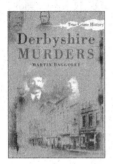

Derbyshire Murders

MARTIN BAGGOLEY

Martin Baggoley revisits ten of the county's most extraordinary and shocking cases from scratch. They include a murder and robbery committed in 1843, and the murder of a police constable in Derby in 1879. Also included are cases from Chaddesden, Chesterfield, Ashbourne, Glossop and Ilkeston. This unique re-examination is sure to appeal to all those interested in the shady side of Derbyshire's past.

978 0 7509 4507 3

Visit our website and discover thousands of other History Press books.**www.thehistorypress.co.uk**